Abraham I

Single & Satisfied

Embracing the Power of Being Single

TABLE OF CONTENTS

ACKNOWLEDGEMNT

I would like to extend my heartfelt gratitude to all those who have played a significant role in the creation of this book, "Single and Satisfied." It is with immense joy and appreciation that I present this vivid acknowledgment.

First and foremost, I express my utmost gratitude to my family and friends who have been my pillars of support throughout this incredible journey. Your unwavering belief in my abilities and continuous encouragement has been instrumental in shaping this book into what it is today.

To my editors, whose meticulous attention to detail and expert guidance has polished the pages of this book and made it shine, I extend my deepest appreciation. Your expertise and dedication have truly made a remarkable difference.

I would also like to extend my gratitude to all the readers and book lovers who will embark on this literary adventure with me. It is your trust and support that continually inspire me to explore the depths of my imagination and share my experiences.

To the literary community and fellow authors, thank you for nurturing a creative environment where ideas are born and flourish. Your passion for storytelling has been a constant source of inspiration throughout my writing process.

Last but certainly not least, I extend my sincere thanks to the AI assistant that has been instrumental in bringing my ideas to life. Your intriguing suggestions, creative input, and clever insights have enriched the pages of this book beyond measure.

"To all the single souls out there, may this book be a source of comfort and empowerment, reminding you that being single is not a mere status but a profound state of contentment and self-discovery. Embrace the journey, cherish your freedom, and dance fearlessly to the rhythm of your heartbeat."

Thank you, one and all, for joining me on this exhilarating adventure, and for helping "Single and Satisfied" come to life.

DEDICATION

To all the resilient souls who have embraced the beauty of their journey.

This book is dedicated to everyone who has learned the profound art of being "single and satisfied."

To those who have discovered that being single is not synonymous with loneliness, but rather an opportunity for growth, self-discovery, and self-love, this dedication is for you.

To the ones who have found contentment in their singlehood, embracing their individuality without compromise or sacrifice.

To all the single hearts who refuse to settle for anything less than they deserve.

And finally, this book is dedicated to the belief that being single can be an incredibly fulfilling and empowering phase of life, one that allows for personal growth, self-discovery, and the nurturing of one's happiness.

INTRODUCTION

In a world where the pursuit of romantic relationships often takes centre stage, it is crucial to recognize the power and potential of being single. "Single and Satisfied: Embracing the Power of Being Single" is a profound exploration of the joys and fulfilment that can be found within the realm of singleness. This book offers guidance, inspiration, and biblical wisdom to empower individuals to embrace their single status, discover their true selves, and live a life of purpose and contentment.

"Single and Satisfied: Embracing the Power of Being Single" redefines singleness as a state of independence, freedom, and self-discovery. It embraces the idea that being single is not a mere absence of a romantic partner but rather an opportunity for personal growth, self-love, and the pursuit of one's passions. This book recognizes the inherent strength and value of being single and aims to shift the narrative to one of empowerment and fulfilment.

"But I want you to be free from concern. One who is unmarried is concerned about the things of the Lord, how he may please the Lord." - 1 Corinthians 7:32

This verse reminds us that singleness provides an opportunity to focus on our relationship with the divine and deepen our spiritual connection. It emphasizes that being single allows for undivided attention to the things that truly matter, enabling us to live a life that is pleasing to God.

"For I know the plans I have for you, declares the Lord, plans to prosper you and not to harm you, plans to give you hope and a future." - Jeremiah 29:11

This powerful verse reassures us that regardless of our relationship status, God has a purpose for our lives. It reminds us that being single does not mean being deprived of a fulfilling future. Instead, it encourages us to trust in God's plans and believe that our single journey is part of a greater divine design.

"Love your neighbor as yourself." - Mark 12:31

This commandment emphasizes the importance of self-love and self-care. It reminds us that being single provides an opportunity to cultivate a deep and compassionate love for ourselves. By embracing self-love, we are better equipped to love and serve others, fostering meaningful connections and relationships.

"Be still before the Lord and wait patiently for him." - Psalm 37:7

This verse encourages us to embrace the stillness and solitude of singleness. It reminds us that this season of waiting can be a time of reflection, self-discovery, and strengthening our faith. By patiently waiting on the Lord, we can cultivate a deeper sense of trust and readiness for the blessings that lie ahead.

"This is the day that the Lord has made; let us rejoice and be glad in it." - Psalm 118:24

This verse serves as a reminder to embrace the present moment and find joy in the journey of singleness. It encourages us to live each day with gratitude, cherishing the opportunities and experiences that come our way. By choosing to rejoice in the present, we unlock the power of being single and cultivate a spirit of contentment and satisfaction.

Single and Satisfied invites readers to embark on a transformative journey of self-discovery, personal growth, and spiritual empowerment through biblical wisdom and inspirational guidance. This book seeks to redefine the meaning of singleness, encouraging individuals to embrace their independence, nurture self-love, and pursue their passions with unwavering confidence. By embracing the power of being single, readers can experience profound satisfaction and live a life that is rooted in purpose, joy, and fulfilment.

PART ONE

EMBRACING SINGLENESS AS A GIFT

"But I want you to be free from concern. One who is unmarried is concerned about the things of the Lord, how he may please the Lord." - 1 Corinthians 7:32

In a world that often emphasizes the importance of romantic relationships and places a premium on being coupled, it is easy for single individuals to feel marginalized or overlooked. However, the journey of singleness is not one to be diminished or disregarded. Instead, it is an opportunity to embrace the unique blessings and possibilities that come with being single. This book, "Single and Satisfied," seeks to shift the narrative surrounding singleness, inviting individuals to recognize and celebrate the inherent value and power of this season of life.

Singleness is not a waiting room for something better, nor is it a state to be endured until the arrival of a romantic partner. Rather, it is a gift, a time to be cherished and fully lived. It is a season of discovery, growth, and self-exploration, where individuals have the freedom to chart their course, pursue their passions, and deepen their relationship with themselves and with God.

In this chapter, we will embark on a journey of exploration, examining the various facets of singleness and uncovering the hidden treasures that lie within. We will challenge societal norms and expectations, questioning their validity and discovering our truths about fulfilment and purpose. We will delve into the depths of personal identity, self-worth, and self-love, understanding that our value is not determined by our relationship status, but by our inherent worth as individuals.

Drawing inspiration from biblical wisdom and timeless truths, we will weave together practical insights, personal stories, and transformative strategies to navigate the challenges and embrace the joys of singleness. Through each segment, we will explore topics such as redefining singleness, seeking divine purpose, cultivating contentment, and embracing personal freedom . We will address common misconceptions, provide tools for self-discovery and personal growth, and offer guidance for navigating the complexities of

Singleness is not a waiting room for something better, nor is it a state to be endured until the arrival of a romantic partner.

relationships and societal pressures.

Throughout this journey, we will be reminded of the powerful biblical quotation from 1 Corinthians 7:32, which states, *"But I want you to be free from concern. One who is unmarried is concerned about the things of the Lord, how he may please the Lord."* These words affirm the inherent beauty and potential of singleness, highlighting the freedom and focus it offers to pursue a deeper relationship with God and to serve His kingdom without distraction.

Whether you are single by choice, circumstance, or season, this book is a companion and guide to help you embrace the gift of singleness wholeheartedly. It is an invitation to celebrate your individuality, pursue your passions, and live a life of purpose and fulfilment.

CHALLENGING SOCIETAL NORMS

Exploring societal expectations and pressures regarding relationships and marriage, and questioning their validity in light of personal fulfilment and spiritual growth.

In a society heavily influenced by cultural norms

and expectations, it is crucial to critically examine the societal pressures and expectations surrounding relationships and marriage. This sub-topic, "Challenging Societal Norms," invites us to explore the prevailing beliefs and stereotypes that often define success, happiness, and fulfilment in terms of being in a romantic partnership. By questioning the validity of these norms and their impact on personal growth and spiritual development, we can pave the way for embracing singleness as a gift.

Societal expectations regarding relationships often convey the message that being single is undesirable or incomplete. The pressure to conform to these norms can lead individuals to view their singleness as a deficiency rather than a valuable opportunity for personal fulfilment and self-discovery. However, by challenging these societal norms, we open the door to redefining our path and embracing the unique advantages that singleness offers.

By questioning the validity of societal expectations, we can liberate ourselves from the pressure to conform and instead focus on what truly brings us joy and fulfilment. It is essential to recognize that

> Singleness allows us the
> freedom to explore our passions,
> deepen our understanding
> of ourselves,
> and pursue our unique purposes
> without compromise.

the pursuit of personal growth, self-discovery, and spiritual connection is not exclusive to being in a romantic relationship. Singleness allows us the freedom to explore our passions, deepen our understanding of ourselves, and pursue our unique purposes without compromise.

By challenging societal norms, we reclaim our autonomy and assert that our worth is not contingent upon our relationship status. We can reject the notion that being single is a deficiency or a failure and instead embrace the idea that singleness offers immense potential for personal growth, self-love, and spiritual transformation.

In light of personal fulfilment and spiritual growth, it is essential to critically evaluate societal expectations and ask ourselves: Do these norms align with our true values and aspirations? Are they supportive of our personal growth and well-being? By questioning these norms, we pave the way for a more authentic and empowering experience of singleness, grounded in our sense of purpose, contentment, and connection with the divine.

As we challenge societal norms, we acknowledge that embracing singleness as a gift requires us to forge our path and define our standards of happiness and fulfilment. We can find solace in knowing that we are not alone in this journey. Many individuals have thrived and found deep satisfaction in their singleness, defying societal expectations and living lives rich in purpose and contentment.

By embarking on this exploration and challenging societal norms, we open ourselves to the possibility of embracing singleness as a true gift. We free ourselves from the constraints of external expectations and pave the way for a more authentic, fulfilling, and spiritually enriching experience of singleness. Ultimately, by challenging societal norms, we empower ourselves to embrace our unique journey and live a life that aligns with our true values, passions, and purpose.

REDEFINING SINGLENESS

Examining the true meaning and value of being single as a time of freedom, self-discovery, and spiritual focus.

In a world that often equates happiness and fulfilment with being in a romantic relationship, it is crucial to redefine the meaning and value of singleness. This sub-topic invites us to delve into the depths of what it truly means to be single and to embrace this season of life as a time of freedom, self-discovery, and spiritual focus.

Singleness is not a state of lack or incompleteness, but rather an opportunity for personal growth and exploration. It is a time to fully embrace our individuality, passions, and dreams without the need for compromise or external validation. By redefining singleness, we shift our perspective from seeing it as a void to be filled, to viewing it as a precious gift to be cherished and maximized.

Being single provides a unique sense of freedom - freedom to make choices and decisions that align with our desires and values. It allows us to prioritize our personal growth, pursue our interests, and invest time and energy into areas that bring us joy and fulfilment. Singleness grants us the freedom to embark on adventures, explore new opportunities, and cultivate a deep sense of self-discovery.

This season of life also presents a remarkable opportunity for spiritual focus. Without the distractions and responsibilities of a romantic relationship, we can devote our time and energy to nurturing our spiritual connection and deepening our relationship with a higher power. Singleness allows us to prioritize our spiritual journey, seeking a deeper understanding of ourselves and the divine.

In embracing singleness as a time of self-discovery, we can uncover our passions, strengths, and weaknesses. We can embark on a journey of self-reflection and introspection, gaining a clearer understanding of our values, goals, and purpose. This self-discovery sets the foundation for personal growth and empowerment, enabling us to step into our true selves and live authentically.

Moreover, singleness offers us the freedom to focus on self-care and personal well-being. It allows us to prioritize our physical, emotional, and

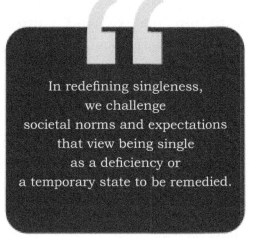

In redefining singleness, we challenge societal norms and expectations that view being single as a deficiency or a temporary state to be remedied.

mental health without compromising the needs and desires of a partner. By nurturing ourselves, we build a strong foundation for future relationships and cultivate a sense of wholeness and contentment in our single state.

In redefining singleness, we challenge societal norms and expectations that view being single as a deficiency or a temporary state to be remedied. We embrace the true essence of singleness as a valuable and purposeful phase of life, filled with opportunities for growth, self-love, and spiritual enrichment.

By examining the true meaning and value of singleness, we open ourselves to the possibilities and potential that this season holds. We shift our focus from the absence of a romantic partner to the abundance of personal growth and fulfilment that can be experienced. In doing so, we reclaim our power, celebrate our individuality, and embrace the freedom, self-discovery, and spiritual focus that singleness can offer.

In the next segments, we will delve deeper into the practical aspects of embracing singleness, exploring the paths to self-love, building meaningful connections, pursuing passions, and finding contentment in the present moment. Together, we will uncover the profound beauty and potential that lie within the embrace of singleness as a gift.

SEEKING DIVINE PURPOSE

Reflecting on how singleness can be viewed as an opportunity to wholeheartedly pursue a deeper relationship with God and discern His plans for one's life.

In our journey as single individuals, it is important to recognize that this season of singleness holds a profound opportunity for us to seek and discover our divine purpose. Rather than viewing singleness as a mere waiting period or a time to be filled with plans of romantic relationships, we can embrace it as a unique and valuable time to wholeheartedly pursue a deeper relationship with God and discern His plans for our lives.

When we intentionally shift our focus from seeking a human partner to seeking a divine connection, we open ourselves to a realm of spiritual growth, revelation, and purpose. Singleness provides us with the precious gift of undivided attention, allowing us to dedicate our time and energy to building a deep and meaningful relationship with our Creator.

In this season, we have the freedom to invest in our spiritual lives without the distractions and demands that can arise in romantic relationships. We can immerse ourselves in prayer, meditation, and the study of sacred texts, delving into the wisdom and teachings that guide us toward a deeper understanding of our identity and purpose. By embracing this opportunity, we create space for divine revelation and guidance to shape our lives.

In seeking divine purpose, we embark on a journey of self-discovery and self-transformation. As we spend time in prayer and reflection, we gain clarity about our passions, talents, and the unique gifts God has bestowed upon us. We begin to discern how these gifts can be used to fulfill His purpose and contribute to the betterment of the world around us.

Through this process, we develop a deeper understanding of our true selves and our place in God's grand design. Singleness becomes a season of exploration, where we can experiment, take risks, and step outside our comfort zones to fulfill the callings that resonate within our hearts. We learn to trust in God's timing and His perfect plan for our lives, knowing that He is faithfully guiding us toward the fulfilment of our divine purpose.

> "
> Singleness becomes a season of exploration, where we can experiment, take risks, and step outside our comfort zones to fulfill the callings that resonate within our hearts.

In the pursuit of divine purpose, we discover that singleness is not a hindrance but rather a fertile ground for spiritual growth and transformation. We cultivate qualities such as patience, faith, and surrender as we surrender our desires and expectations to the will of God. We learn to rely on His guidance and seek His wisdom in every aspect of our lives.

Moreover, the deepening relationship with God that comes with embracing singleness as a time to seek divine purpose serves as a firm foundation for any future relationship. By developing a strong spiritual connection, we enter into potential partnerships from a place of wholeness, allowing God to guide our choices and align our lives with His will.

As we reflect on singleness as an opportunity to seek divine purpose, we recognize that this season is not one to be endured but rather embraced and celebrated. It is a time to invest in our relationship with God, align our hearts with His plans, and discover the unique calling He has placed upon our lives.

In the following segments, we will explore practical ways to deepen our spiritual connection, discern God's guidance, and live out our divine purpose in the context of singleness. Together, we will embark on a journey of seeking and embracing the profound purpose that awaits us in this sacred season of our lives.

DEVELOPING SPIRITUAL INTIMACY

Exploring the unique advantages of being single in fostering a deep and intimate connection with God, allowing for undivided attention to spiritual growth and service.

In the journey of singleness, there lies a remarkable advantage—an opportunity to develop a profound and intimate spiritual connection with God. This sub-topic, "Developing Spiritual Intimacy," invites us to explore the unique advantages that being single provides in fostering a deep and meaningful relationship with our Creator. It acknowledges the undivided attention and freedom to dedicate ourselves to spiritual growth and service that singleness offers.

As single individuals, we have the precious gift of uninterrupted time and space to cultivate our spiritual lives. Without the demands and responsibilities that come with a romantic partnership, we can devote ourselves wholeheartedly to seeking and developing a deep intimacy with God. We have the freedom to prioritize our spiritual growth, nurture our faith, and engage in practices that foster a strong and vibrant connection with the divine.

Being single allows us to allocate our time and energy solely toward our spiritual journey. We can invest in practices such as prayer, meditation, contemplation, and the study of sacred texts without the distractions that may arise in the context of a romantic relationship. This undivided attention enables us to deepen our understanding of God's nature, His teachings, and His will for our lives.

In the solitude of singleness, we can carve out sacred spaces and moments for communion with God. We have the freedom to create a rhythm of spiritual disciplines and practices that resonate with our souls, allowing us to grow closer to our Creator. This focused attention opens doors to profound revelations, guidance, and transformative encounters with the divine.

Moreover, being single grants us the flexibility to engage in acts of service and ministry with greater dedication and availability. We can devote our time and resources to supporting and uplifting others, recognizing that our singleness provides an

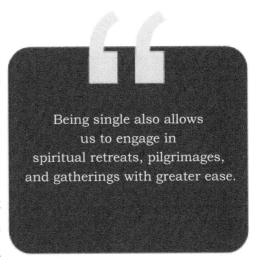

Being single also allows us to engage in spiritual retreats, pilgrimages, and gatherings with greater ease.

opportunity to extend love and compassion to those in need. By serving others, we deepen our connection with God and align ourselves with His heart for justice, mercy, and reconciliation.

Being single also allows us to engage in spiritual retreats, pilgrimages, and gatherings with greater ease. We have the freedom to embark on journeys of self-discovery and spiritual exploration, immersing ourselves in transformative experiences that open our hearts to the presence of the divine. These encounters with different spiritual traditions, communities, and practices enrich our spiritual journey, expanding our understanding of God's diverse manifestations in the world.

In the context of singleness, we can embrace

solitude as a sacred space for encountering God. The absence of a romantic partner does not equate to loneliness but rather invites us to embrace the solitude that allows for deep introspection, reflection, and communion with the divine. In these moments of stillness and solitude, we discover that we are never alone, for God's presence is ever near, comforting, and guiding us.

As we develop spiritual intimacy in our singleness, we find solace, strength, and purpose. We experience a profound sense of connection with the divine that transcends human relationships and temporal circumstances. It is in this deep intimacy with God that we find fulfilment, peace, and a profound sense of belonging.

As we proceed, we will delve deeper into practical ways to foster spiritual intimacy, including cultivating a daily spiritual practice, engaging in acts of service, participating in spiritual communities, and embracing solitude and silence. Together, we will explore the immeasurable advantages that singleness offers in developing a rich, intimate relationship with God and discovering our unique role in His grand tapestry of creation.

PRIORITIZING KINGDOM WORK

Embracing singleness as a time to dedicate oneself to serving God's kingdom without the distractions and responsibilities of a romantic relationship or family obligations.

In the journey of singleness, we are presented with a unique opportunity to prioritize and dedicate ourselves wholeheartedly to serving God's kingdom. This sub-topic, "Prioritizing Kingdom Work," invites us to explore the advantages of being single in terms of our ability to focus on advancing God's purposes without the distractions and responsibilities that may come with a romantic relationship or family obligations.

Singleness provides us with a season of life where we can fully immerse ourselves in serving God's kingdom without the constraints of divided attention or conflicting priorities. With fewer external obligations, we have the freedom to engage in various forms of ministry, mission, and service. We can dedicate our time, energy, and resources to advancing the cause of Christ and spreading His love and truth to those around us.

By embracing singleness as a time to prioritize

kingdom work, we acknowledge that our primary focus is on fulfilling God's purposes and expanding His kingdom rather than solely pursuing personal desires or romantic relationships. We recognize that this season offers us the unique advantage of undivided attention and availability to engage in service, evangelism, discipleship, and other forms of ministry.

Singleness allows us to fully devote ourselves to God's work, aligning our lives with His mission and purpose. We can embrace opportunities for spiritual growth, leadership development, and impactful service that may require significant time and effort. We have the freedom to say "yes" to God's calling without the need for extensive consultation or consideration of the needs and responsibilities of a partner or family.

In the context of singleness, we have the flexibility to explore different forms of ministry and serve in various capacities. We can embark on mission trips, volunteer for charitable organizations, engage in community outreach, and participate in discipleship programs. The absence of romantic or family commitments allows us to respond to the needs and opportunities that arise in the world

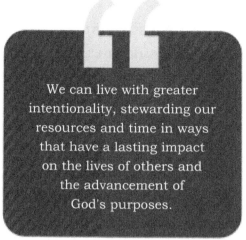

> We can live with greater intentionality, stewarding our resources and time in ways that have a lasting impact on the lives of others and the advancement of God's purposes.

with greater agility and availability.

Singleness also enables us to build deep relationships within the body of Christ, fostering spiritual community, and partnering with fellow believers in advancing God's kingdom. We can invest in mentoring relationships, discipleship, and supporting the growth and development of others. The freedom to cultivate these meaningful connections contributes to our spiritual growth and the strengthening of the church as a whole.

Moreover, singleness grants us the freedom to embrace a lifestyle of simplicity and sacrifice to prioritize kingdom work. We can make choices that align with the values of God's kingdom rather than being tied down by the responsibilities and financial obligations that often accompany relationships and family life. We can live with greater intentionality, stewarding our resources and time in ways that have a lasting impact on the lives of others and the advancement of God's purposes.

As we embrace singleness as a time to prioritize kingdom work, we recognize that our service is not motivated by a sense of duty or obligation, but rather by a deep love for God and a desire to participate in His redemptive work in the world. We understand that our singleness is not a limitation but a unique opportunity to wholeheartedly dedicate ourselves to the transformative work of God's kingdom.

CULTIVATING CONTENTMENT

Discovering the key to finding contentment and fulfilment in the present moment as a single individual, rather than waiting for a relationship to bring happiness.

In a society that often places a high value on romantic relationships and marriage, it can be challenging for single individuals to cultivate a sense of contentment and fulfilment in their current season of life. However, this sub-topic, "Cultivating Contentment," invites us to explore the key to finding true contentment and happiness as single individuals, rather than waiting for a relationship to make us fulfilled.

Contentment is a state of being where we are at peace with ourselves, our circumstances, and our relationship with God. It is not dependent on external factors such as relationship status but rather springs from an inner acceptance and gratitude for the present moment. As single individuals, we have the opportunity to discover and embrace the keys to cultivating contentment, which enable us to experience joy and fulfilment in our lives, irrespective of our relationship status.

The first key to cultivating contentment is shifting our perspective and embracing the belief that singleness is not a deficiency or a waiting period, but a unique and valuable season of life. It is a time of growth, self-discovery, and personal development. By reframing our mindset, we can view singleness as an opportunity rather than a limitation, recognizing that our worth and happiness are not dependent on being in a romantic relationship.

In addition, cultivating contentment requires us to develop a deep sense of self-love and self-acceptance. We must learn to appreciate and value ourselves as individuals, recognizing our inherent worth and the unique qualities we bring to the world. This involves practicing self-care, setting healthy boundaries, and nurturing our physical, emotional, and spiritual well-being. When we love and accept ourselves, we are better equipped to find contentment and extend that love to others.

Another key to finding contentment as a single individual is cultivating gratitude. Gratitude shifts our focus from what we lack to what we have been blessed with in our lives. It allows us to appreciate the present moment and the blessings that come with it. By cultivating a daily practice of gratitude, we train our minds to see the abundance and goodness that surrounds us, fostering a sense of contentment and appreciation for the blessings of our singleness. Furthermore, cultivating contentment

> "Gratitude shifts our focus from what we lack to what we have been blessed with in our lives.

involves embracing the freedom and opportunities that come with being single. We have the freedom to pursue our passions, explore our interests, and invest in personal growth and self-discovery. This season provides us with the space and flexibility to pursue dreams, goals, and aspirations without the constraints of a romantic relationship or family responsibilities. Embracing this freedom empowers us to find contentment and fulfilment in the pursuit of our individual paths.

A crucial aspect of cultivating contentment is deepening our relationship with God. As single individuals, we have a unique opportunity to draw near to God and find our ultimate fulfilment and satisfaction in Him. By seeking God's presence, studying His Word, and spending time in prayer and meditation, we open ourselves to experiencing His love, peace, and joy in profound ways. This spiritual connection becomes a source of contentment and fulfilment that transcends the temporal circumstances of our singleness.

In the journey of cultivating contentment, it is important to remember that it is not a one-time accomplishment but an ongoing practice. It requires intentionality, self-reflection, and a willingness to surrender our desires and expectations to God. It is a process of learning to find joy, fulfilment, and purpose in the present moment, trusting that God's plan for our lives is perfect and that He has a unique purpose for our singleness.

OVERCOMING STIGMA AND MISCONCEPTIONS

Addressing common misconceptions and negative stereotypes surrounding singleness, and learning to embrace the inherent worth and dignity of being single.

In today's society, singleness is often accompanied by misconceptions, negative stereotypes, and a certain degree of stigma. Many individuals face external pressures and internal struggles due to the societal expectations and judgments associated with being single. However, this sub-topic, "Overcoming Stigma and Misconceptions," encourages us to address and challenge these misconceptions, as well as embrace the inherent worth and dignity of being single.

One of the common misconceptions surrounding singleness is the belief that it is a state of incompleteness or loneliness. Society often suggests that true fulfilment can only be found within the context of a romantic relationship or marriage. However, it is essential to recognize that singleness is not synonymous with loneliness or lacking something. It is a valid and valuable way of living, filled with opportunities for growth, self-discovery, and meaningful connections.

Another misconception is the assumption that single individuals are somehow flawed or undesirable. Society may perpetuate the idea that those who are single must be lacking in some way, leading to self-doubt and a diminished sense of self-worth. However, it is crucial to challenge this belief and affirm the inherent worth and dignity of being single. Our relationship status does not define our value as individuals. Each person is unique, valuable, and worthy of love and respect, regardless of their relationship status.

There can be a stigma attached to singleness as if it is a temporary condition that needs to be fixed or resolved. Society may view singleness as a problem to be solved rather than a valid and fulfilling way of life. This perspective can create pressure and a sense of inadequacy for single individuals.

However, it is important to recognize that singleness is not a problem in need of a solution. It is a valid life choice or circumstance that can bring joy, purpose, and fulfilment.

Addressing these misconceptions and overcoming stigma begins with self-acceptance and self-empowerment. As single individuals, it is essential to embrace and celebrate our unique journey. We must affirm our worth, reject negative stereotypes, and challenge societal expectations that undermine our sense of self. This involves cultivating a positive self-image, practicing self-compassion, and surrounding ourselves with supportive and affirming communities.

Moreover, overcoming stigma and misconceptions requires open and honest conversations about singleness. By engaging in dialogue, sharing our experiences, and challenging societal norms, we can foster a more inclusive and understanding perspective. This dialogue can help to break down stereotypes, educate others about the value of singleness, and promote acceptance and respect for diverse paths in life.

It is also important to create spaces and communities where single individuals feel seen, heard, and valued. Building supportive networks of friends, family, and like-minded individuals can provide a sense of belonging and affirmation. These communities can celebrate the unique joys and challenges of singleness and offer support and encouragement in navigating societal pressures and misconceptions.

Additionally, educating ourselves and others about the diverse experiences and contributions of single individuals can help to challenge stereotypes and broaden perspectives. By highlighting the achievements, talents, and positive impact of single individuals in various fields and areas of life, we can shift the narrative surrounding singleness and promote a more inclusive and respectful society.

Ultimately, overcoming stigma and misconceptions is about recognizing and embracing the inherent worth and dignity of being single. It is about understanding that our value as individuals is not determined by our relationship status but by our character, passions, contributions, and the love and acceptance we extend to ourselves and others. By challenging societal norms and embracing the fullness of our lives as single individuals, we can break free from the shackles of stigma

EMBRACING PERSONAL FREEDOM

Recognizing the unique opportunities for personal growth, self-care, and self-discovery that singleness affords, allowing individuals to fully embrace their individuality and pursue their passions.

One of the remarkable aspects of singleness is the personal freedom it provides. It offers a season of life where individuals have the unique opportunity to focus on personal growth, self-care, and self-discovery. This sub-topic, "Embracing Personal Freedom," invites us to explore the various ways in which singleness allows individuals to fully embrace their individuality, pursue their passions, and nurture their well-being.

Singleness grants individuals the freedom to cultivate their identity and embrace their individuality. Without the obligations and compromises that come with a romantic relationship or family responsibilities, single individuals have the liberty to explore their interests, values, and beliefs. They can delve into self-reflection, discovering their true passions, strengths, and purpose. This freedom allows for a deeper understanding of oneself and the opportunity to build a strong foundation for personal growth and fulfilment.

Moreover, being single provides the space and time for self-care and self-nurturing. Individuals can prioritize their physical, emotional, and spiritual well-being without the distractions or demands of a romantic relationship. They can engage in activities that bring them joy, practice healthy habits, and invest in activities that promote their overall well-being. Whether it's pursuing hobbies, engaging in fitness, practicing mindfulness, or nurturing spiritual practices, singleness allows for a dedicated focus on self-care and self-development.

> being single provides the space and time for self-care and self-nurturing.

Singleness also affords individuals the opportunity to embark on a journey of self-discovery. It is a time to explore new experiences, take risks, and step out of one's comfort zone. Without the need for constant compromise or consideration of a partner's preferences, single individuals can fully immerse themselves in new endeavours, travel, education, and personal growth opportunities. This journey of self-discovery allows individuals to unearth their passions, expand their horizons, and shape their lives according to their aspirations and dreams.

In addition, the personal freedom of singleness provides the flexibility to pursue professional goals and ambitions. Single individuals have the ability to dedicate time and energy to their careers, pursue higher education, or invest in entrepreneurial endeavours. They can take on challenging projects, seek out new opportunities for advancement, and make decisions that align with their professional aspirations. This freedom allows for a focused pursuit of professional excellence and the fulfilment that comes with achieving one's goals.

In the context of personal freedom, singleness also opens doors for meaningful connections and relationships beyond the realm of romantic partnerships. Single individuals have the opportunity to build a diverse network of friendships, mentorships, and communities. They can invest in deep and meaningful relationships that enrich their lives, provide support, and foster personal growth. These connections offer a sense of belonging, camaraderie, and shared experiences, contributing to a fulfilling and well-rounded life.

As single individuals embrace personal freedom, they develop a sense of autonomy, self-confidence, and resilience. They become comfortable and learn to rely on themselves for happiness and fulfilment. This self-assuredness allows for healthy boundaries, effective decision-making, and the ability to navigate life's challenges with grace and strength.

NAVIGATING LONELINESS

Addressing the challenges of loneliness that can arise in singleness and discovering healthy coping mechanisms, building a support system, and finding solace in God's presence.

While singleness offers many opportunities for personal growth and freedom, it can also come with its share of challenges, including the experience of loneliness. Loneliness is a common human emotion that can be intensified during periods of singleness when individuals desire companionship and connection. This sub-topic, "Navigating Loneliness," invites us to acknowledge and address the challenges of loneliness in singleness, explore healthy coping mechanisms, build a support system, and find solace in God's presence.

Loneliness is not solely determined by one's relationship status but is a universal human experience that can be present in various seasons of life. However, it is essential to acknowledge that singleness can amplify feelings of loneliness, particularly when societal expectations and cultural norms emphasize the importance of romantic relationships. Recognizing and validating these emotions is an important first step in navigating loneliness.

In navigating loneliness, it is crucial to develop healthy coping mechanisms that promote emotional well-being. This may include engaging in activities that bring joy and fulfilment, such as pursuing hobbies, volunteering, or participating in social or community events. Engaging in these activities allows individuals to connect with others who share similar interests, fosterin g a sense of belonging and companionship. Building a support system is another vital aspect of navigating loneliness. This can involve

> relationships provide sense of companionship, emotional support, and understanding, alleviating feelings of isolation.

cultivating meaningful friendships, fostering connections with family members, or seeking support from communities or support groups specifically designed for single individuals. These relationships provide a sense of companionship, emotional support, and understanding, alleviating feelings of isolation. Sharing experiences, seeking advice, and offering mutual encouragement within a supportive community can make the journey of singleness more bearable.

In addition to building a support system, finding solace in God's presence can bring profound comfort and strength. Recognizing that God is a loving and compassionate companion who walks alongside us in every season of life can provide solace and a sense of belonging. Through prayer, meditation, and reflection on God's Word, individuals can experience a deep and intimate connection with the Divine, finding solace in His unwavering presence. Drawing near to God in times of loneliness allows for spiritual nourishment, a renewed sense of purpose, and the assurance that we are never truly alone.

It is also important to cultivate self-compassion and self-care when navigating loneliness. Practicing self-compassion involves treating oneself with kindness, understanding, and acceptance, rather than self-judgment or criticism. Engaging in self-care activities that prioritize one's physical, emotional, and spiritual well-being can help combat feelings of loneliness. This may include practicing mindfulness, engaging in regular exercise, seeking professional counselling or therapy, or participating in activities that promote self-reflection and personal growth.

Don't forget that navigating loneliness is not a linear journey, and there may be moments when it feels more challenging than others. However, by acknowledging these emotions, seeking support, and finding solace in God's presence, individuals can navigate the challenges of loneliness with resilience, grace, and hope.

BUILDING A STRONG FOUNDATION

Exploring the importance of establishing a solid foundation of self-worth, self-love, and personal identity as a single individual, rooted in God's unconditional love and acceptance.

In the journey of singleness, building a strong foundation is essential for navigating the various challenges and embracing the joys that come with this season of life. This sub-topic, "Building a Strong Foundation," invites us to explore the significance of establishing a solid sense of self-worth, self-love, and personal identity as single individuals, all rooted in God's unconditional love and acceptance.

Often, societal norms and cultural expectations place a heavy emphasis on the value of romantic relationships, which can inadvertently undermine the importance of self-worth and personal identity. However, as single individuals, it is vital to recognize that our worth is not contingent upon our relationship status or the opinions of others. Our worth is intrinsic and comes from being children of God, created in His image and deeply loved by Him.

Building a strong foundation begins with developing a healthy sense of self-worth. This involves recognizing and appreciating our unique qualities, strengths, and talents. It is about embracing our imperfections and celebrating the inherent value we bring to the world. Understanding that we are fearfully and wonderfully made allows us to cultivate a positive self-image and a deep appreciation for who we are as individuals.

Self-love is another critical component of building a strong foundation. It means treating ourselves with kindness, compassion, and respect. It involves prioritizing self-care, setting healthy boundaries, and engaging in practices that nurture our physical, emotional, and spiritual well-being. Self-love allows us to recognize our needs and desires, and to invest in our growth, happiness, and fulfilment.

Central to building a strong foundation as single individuals is establishing a clear personal identity. This includes understanding our values, passions, and life goals. It involves embracing our unique purpose and calling, independent of a romantic relationship. Discovering our passions, pursuing our dreams, and actively engaging in activities that align with our values contribute to a sense of fulfilment and a solid personal identity.

Anchoring this foundation in God's unconditional love and acceptance provides a solid and unshakable source of affirmation and security. The Scriptures remind us of God's deep love for each of us, regardless of our relationship status. For example, in Jeremiah 31:3, it is written, "I have loved you with an everlasting love." Understanding and internalizing this truth allows us to find comfort and strength in God's presence, knowing that His love for us is unwavering and unconditional.

By rooting our self-worth, self-love, and personal identity in God's love and acceptance, we find freedom from the opinions and judgments of others. We are no longer defined by societal expectations or cultural norms, but by the truth of our identity as beloved children of God. This foundation empowers us to embrace our singleness with confidence, joy, and purpose.

I would also like to extend my gratitude to all the readers and book lovers who will embark on this literary adventure with me. It is your trust and support that continually inspire me to explore the depths of my imagination and share my experiences.

PART TWO

SELF-DISCOVERY AND PERSONAL GROWTH

"For I know the plans I have for you, declares the Lord, plans to prosper you and not to harm you, plans to give you hope and a future." - Jeremiah 29:11

INTRODUCTION

In the journey of singleness lies a vast landscape of self-discovery and personal growth. It is a season brimming with opportunities to explore the depths of our being, unravel our true passions, and embark on a transformative journey of self-understanding and fulfilment. This segment, "Self-Discovery and Personal Growth," delves into the rich terrain of self-exploration, guiding individuals towards uncovering their unique identities and embracing the limitless potential that resides within them.

In a world that often defines our worth by external measures, such as relationship status or achievements, it is easy to lose sight of our authentic selves. Singleness, however, provides a fertile ground for self-discovery, where we can peel back the layers of societal expectations and delve into the core of our being. It is a time to ask ourselves the fundamental questions that lead to a deeper understanding of who we are, what brings us joy, and how we can contribute meaningfully to the world around us.

Self-discovery is not a linear process but a journey of exploration and curiosity. It is about becoming attuned to our inner voice, our passions, and our values. Through self-reflection and introspection, we can uncover our true desires and aspirations, unlocking a sense of purpose that goes beyond societal definitions. It is through this process that we begin to recognize the unique gifts and talents we possess and discover how they can be cultivated and shared with the world.

Personal growth is an integral part of the self-discovery journey. As we gain insights into our authentic selves, we are called to nurture and develop our potential. This involves engaging in intentional practices that promote growth, such as expanding our knowledge, acquiring new skills, and embracing challenges that stretch our boundaries. It also entails confronting our fears and limitations, allowing us to evolve into the best version of ourselves.

In the pursuit of

> "
> Through self-reflection and introspection, we can uncover our true desires and aspirations, unlocking a sense of purpose that goes beyond societal definitions.

self-discovery and personal growth, we are reminded of the profound biblical quotation found in Jeremiah 29:11, which states, *"For I know the plans I have for you, declares the Lord, plans to prosper you and not to harm you, plans to give you hope and a future."* This verse reassures us that God has a purpose and a plan for our lives, filled with hope and a future. It instils in us the confidence to embrace the journey of self-discovery, knowing that we are not alone and that God is intimately involved in our growth and transformation.

Throughout this segment, we will explore practical strategies, tools, and insights to facilitate self-discovery and personal growth. We will delve into the power of introspection, mindfulness, and self-care practices that nourish our minds, bodies, and spirits. We will also examine the importance of embracing our passions and stepping outside our comfort zones to unlock our full potential.

By embarking on the path of self-discovery and personal growth, we not only deepen our understanding of ourselves but also enhance our capacity to navigate relationships, pursue meaningful endeavours, and make a positive impact in the world. This segment serves as a guide, encouraging individuals to embark on a transformative journey of self-exploration and embracing the boundless possibilities that lie within. Let us uncover our true selves, embrace our unique identities, and step into a future filled with purpose, joy, and fulfilment.

EMBRACING THE JOURNEY OF SELF-DISCOVERY

In the depths of our souls lies a longing to understand ourselves fully and to live a life of purpose and meaning. The journey of self-discovery is an invitation to embark on this transformative quest, a path that leads us to uncover the essence of who we truly are. It is a journey that takes us beyond the surface-level identities imposed by society and delves into the depths of our being, where our passions, strengths, and authentic selves reside.

Self-discovery is not a destination; it is a continuous process that unfolds throughout our lives. It is a journey of self-exploration, introspection, and reflection that allows us to peel back the layers of conditioning, expectations, and influences that have shaped us. It invites us to question our beliefs, examine our values, and embrace our unique qualities and aspirations.

When we embark on the journey of self-discovery, we open ourselves up to a world of possibilities. We gain clarity about our passions, interests, and talents, enabling us to align our lives with what truly brings us joy and fulfilment. Through self-discovery, we uncover the hidden depths of our souls and find the courage to live authentically, free from the shackles of societal expectations and pressures.

This journey is not always easy. It requires introspection, self-reflection, and a willingness to confront our fears, doubts, and vulnerabilities. It demands that we let go of old narratives and stories that no longer serve us, and embrace new perspectives that align with our true selves. But the rewards are immeasurable. Self-discovery brings us closer to our purpose, allowing us to live lives of authenticity, passion, and alignment with our deepest values.

"For I know the plans I have for you, declares the Lord, plans to prosper you and not to harm you, plans to give you hope and a future." -

Jeremiah 29:11

As we embark on the journey of self-discovery, we are reminded of God's plans for us. He knows us intimately and has designed a unique path for each of us. The biblical quotation from Jeremiah 29:11 assures us that God's plans are for our prosperity, not harm, and that they offer hope and a future. In our pursuit of self-discovery, we can trust that God walks beside us, guiding us toward our true selves and purpose.

So, let us embrace the journey of self-discovery with open hearts and minds. Let us embark on this transformative quest to uncover our authentic identities, passions, and purpose. As we delve into the depths of our souls, may we discover the true essence of who we are and live lives of authenticity, meaning, and purpose.

THE ESSENCE OF SELF-DISCOVERY

Through self-discovery, we gain a deeper understanding of who we are at our core and what truly matters to us. It is a journey of self-exploration that allows us to shed the masks we wear and embrace our authentic selves.

Self-discovery is a courageous act of self-reflection and introspection. It requires us to question the narratives and beliefs that have been ingrained in us and to challenge societal norms and expectations. It invites us to explore our passions and interests, to identify our unique strengths and talents, and to confront our fears and limitations.

During the process of self-discovery, we begin to recognize the patterns and behaviours that no longer serve us. We become aware of the areas of our lives where we feel inauthentic or unfulfilled. It is through this awareness that we can make conscious choices to align our lives with our true selves and pursue paths that bring us joy, purpose, and fulfilment.

Self-discovery also involves embracing vulnerability and embracing the unknown. It requires us to step outside of our comfort zones and explore new territories, both internally and externally. It is in these moments of vulnerability and exploration that we often find the greatest opportunities for growth and self-realization.

The impact of self-discovery on our lives is profound. As we gain a deeper understanding of ourselves, we develop a stronger sense of self-worth and self-acceptance. We learn to honour our needs and desires, setting boundaries that align with our values and priorities. Self-discovery empowers us to

> self-discovery opens the door to personal growth and transformation.

make choices that are authentic and true to ourselves, rather than seeking validation or approval from others.

Moreover, self-discovery opens the door to personal growth and transformation. It allows us to identify areas for improvement and to cultivate new skills and perspectives. As we become more self-aware, we are better equipped to navigate life's challenges and make conscious decisions that lead to personal and professional success.

"For I know the plans I have for you, declares the Lord, plans to prosper you and not to harm you, plans to give you hope and a future." - Jeremiah 29:11

Jeremiah 29:11 reminds us that self-discovery is part of God's plan for our lives. He desires our prosperity, and He has placed within us the potential for growth and fulfilment. Through self-discovery, we align ourselves with God's purpose for us, uncovering the unique gifts and talents He has bestowed upon us.

In conclusion, self-discovery is a transformative journey that invites us to peel back the layers of societal conditioning and uncover our true selves. It is a courageous act of self-reflection and introspection that leads to greater self-awareness, self-acceptance, and personal growth. By embracing self-discovery, we align ourselves with God's plan for our lives and unlock our full potential. Let us embark on this journey with curiosity, openness, and a willingness to embrace the essence of who we truly are.

EMBRACING AUTHENTICITY

In a world that often encourages conformity and masks our true identities, embracing authenticity is a revolutionary act of self-empowerment and personal freedom. It is the process of wholeheartedly embracing and expressing our true selves, without fear or shame. When we live authentically, we align with our core values, honour our unique experiences, and foster deep connections with others. In this segment, we will explore the importance of embracing authenticity on our journey of self-discovery and personal growth.

Defining Authenticity:

Authenticity is the state of being genuine, true, and aligned with our innermost selves. It is about embracing our strengths, vulnerabilities, quirks, and imperfections, without the need for preteens or façade. Authenticity requires us to be honest and transparent, both with ourselves and with others. It is an unwavering commitment to living in alignment with our values, beliefs, and passions, rather than conforming to external expectations or seeking validation from others.

The Power of Authentic Living:

When we embrace authenticity, we tap into our personal power and unlock our true potential. By honouring our authentic selves, we give ourselves permission to live a life that is congruent with who we truly are. This empowers us to make choices, pursue goals, and engage in relationships that align with our values and aspirations. Authentic living allows us to break free from societal constraints and discover a deep sense of fulfilment, joy, and purpose.

The Power of Authenticity:

Authenticity is a powerful force that allows us to show up as our true selves in all aspects of life. By embracing authenticity, we honour our unique identities and recognize that our worth is not dependent on external validation. It empowers us to live in alignment with our values and make choices that are true to our souls.

Liberating from Societal Expectations:

Society often imposes expectations and norms upon us, influencing how we should look, behave, and live our lives. Embracing authenticity requires breaking free from these constraints and embracing our true identities, regardless of societal pressures. It is about living a life that is true to ourselves, even if it means going against the grain

Overcoming Fear and Vulnerability:

Embracing authenticity requires us to confront our fears and embrace vulnerability. It can be intimidating to show up as our true selves, as it exposes us to potential judgment or rejection. However, when we acknowledge and embrace our vulnerabilities, we create opportunities for genuine connections and authentic relationships. It is through vulnerability that we invite others to see us for who we truly are and foster deep, meaningful connections based on trust and understanding.

Aligning with Our Core Values:

Living authentically means aligning our actions and choices with our core values. It requires us to reflect on what truly matters to us and make decisions that are in line with our deepest beliefs. When we live in alignment with our values, we experience a sense of integrity, purpose, and fulfilment. Our lives become a reflection of our true selves, and we attract experiences and relationships that are congruent with who we are. Embracing authenticity means living in alignment with our deepest values. It requires us to reflect on what truly matters to us and make choices that reflect those values. By aligning our actions with our values, we create a sense of congruence and integrity in our lives.

Embracing Imperfections and Growth:
Authenticity embraces the beauty of imperfection and recognizes that growth and self-discovery are ongoing processes. It invites us to accept ourselves fully, including our flaws and mistakes, while also being open to learning, evolving, and embracing new experiences. Embracing authenticity means embracing our unique journey and allowing ourselves room for growth, self-compassion, and personal development.

"So God created mankind in his own image, in the image of God he created them; male and female he created them." - Genesis 1:27

The biblical quotation from Genesis 1:27 reminds us of our divine origin and inherent worth. It affirms that we are created in the image of God, each with our unique qualities and identities. Embracing authenticity is an act of honouring the divine spark within us and living in alignment with the truth of who we are.

Cultivating Self-Expression:

Authenticity is closely linked to self-expression. It involves expressing our thoughts, emotions, and beliefs honestly and authentically. By embracing our authentic voices, we invite others to do the same and create spaces for genuine connections and understanding.

Cultivating Meaningful Connections:

Authenticity paves the way for meaningful connections with others. When we show up authentically, we attract people who appreciate us for who we truly are. Authentic connections are built on trust, vulnerability, and mutual acceptance.

Embracing authenticity is a transformative journey that invites us to embrace and express our true selves. It is a powerful act of self-acceptance, empowerment, and personal freedom. When we live authentically, we align with our core values, honour our unique experiences, and foster deep connections with others. It is through authenticity that we can truly embrace self-discovery, personal growth, and a life of fulfilment and purpose. May we have the courage to embrace authenticity and live in alignment with our

The Transformative Power of Self-Reflection:
Self-reflection indeed holds transformative power in the realm of self-discovery and personal growth. It is a process that involves introspection, mindful observation, and often, journaling, all of which contribute to gaining profound insights into our thoughts, emotions, and behavioural patterns. By engaging in self-reflection, we embark on a journey of understanding ourselves on a deeper level, unravelling hidden beliefs, and making conscious choices that align with our true and authentic selves.

One of the key benefits of self-reflection is gaining self-awareness. Through introspection, we develop an ability to observe our thoughts, emotions, and actions without judgment. This heightened self-awareness allows us to recognize our strengths and weaknesses, understand our values and priorities, and identify areas where personal growth is needed. By gaining clarity about who we are and what truly matters to us, we can make more intentional decisions and navigate our lives in a way that is aligned with our authentic selves.

Self-reflection also helps us uncover hidden beliefs and assumptions that shape our perspectives and behaviour. Often, we operate on autopilot, driven by unconscious patterns and conditioned responses. By taking the time to reflect on our experiences and actions, we can start to question these underlying beliefs and challenge the assumptions that may no longer serve us. This process of self-inquiry allows us to break free from limiting beliefs, expand our perspectives, and open ourselves to new possibilities.

Furthermore, self-reflection enables us to cultivate self-compassion and self-acceptance. Through mindful observation of our thoughts and emotions, we develop a compassionate and non-judgmental attitude towards ourselves. This compassionate stance allows us to acknowledge our flaws and imperfections without self-criticism, fostering a sense of self-acceptance and nurturing a positive self-image. As we deepen our self-compassion, we also become more understanding and empathetic towards others, enhancing our relationships and connections with those around us.

Journaling is a powerful tool that often complements self-reflection. Writing down our thoughts, feelings, and experiences provides a tangible outlet for self-expression and introspection. Journaling allows us to track our personal growth over time, identify recurring patterns, and gain clarity on complex emotions or challenging situations. The act of writing helps organize our thoughts and can often lead to new insights or perspectives that may have remained hidden otherwise.

In conclusion, self-reflection is a transformative process that facilitates self-discovery, personal growth, and living in alignment with our authentic selves. By engaging in introspection, mindful observation, and journaling, we gain self-awareness, uncover hidden beliefs, and develop self-compassion. Through self-reflection, we can make conscious choices and navigate our lives in a way that brings us closer to fulfilment, purpose, and genuine happiness.

EMBRACING CHANGE AND GROWTH

Embracing change and growth is indeed an integral part of the journey of self-discovery. It involves venturing into uncharted territories and stepping outside our comfort zones, which can bring about discomfort and challenges. However, it is through these experiences that we open ourselves up to new opportunities, perspectives, and possibilities for personal growth and transformation.

One of the main reasons why change and growth can be uncomfortable is because they disrupt our familiar routines and patterns. Humans are creatures of habit, and we often find comfort in the familiar and predictable. Stepping into the unknown requires us to let go of the security provided by our comfort zones and embrace uncertainty. It may involve facing fears, confronting limitations, or challenging long-held beliefs. This discomfort, however, is a natural part of the process of growth and should be seen as an opportunity for expansion rather than a reason to retreat.

Embracing change and growth also means being open to new experiences and perspectives. It requires a willingness to explore different paths, ideas, and ways of being. This openness allows us to broaden our horizons and break free from narrow-mindedness. It enables us to learn from others, question our assumptions, and gain new insights. By embracing change, we create space for personal evolution and develop a more flexible and adaptable mind-set.

It is important to note that growth often occurs outside of our comfort zones. When we challenge ourselves and take risks, we discover hidden strengths, capabilities, and passions that we may have never known existed. By pushing ourselves beyond what is familiar and comfortable, we expand our limits and tap into our true potential. Growth also involves learning from failures and setbacks, as they provide valuable lessons and opportunities for resilience and self-reflection.

Moreover, embracing change and growth requires patience and self-compassion. Personal transformation is a gradual process that unfolds over time. It is essential to be kind to ourselves and recognize that change does not happen overnight. It is natural to encounter obstacles, setbacks, and moments of self-doubt along the way. By cultivating self-compassion and practicing resilience, we can navigate these challenges with grace and perseverance.

In summary, embracing change and growth is an integral part of the journey of self-discovery. Although it can be uncomfortable and challenging, it opens the door to new experiences, perspectives, and possibilities for personal growth and transformation. By stepping outside our comfort zones, we expand our limits, learn from failures, and tap into our true potential. With patience, self-compassion, and a willingness to embrace the unknown, we can embark on a transformative path of self-exploration and growth.

CULTIVATING SELF-COMPASSION

Self-compassion is a crucial component of the self-discovery journey. We will discuss the importance of treating ourselves with kindness, understanding, and acceptance as we navigate the highs and lows of self-exploration. Through self-compassion, we can nurture our inner selves and develop resilience in the face of self-discovery's inherent challenges.

"For I know the plans I have for you, declares the Lord, plans to prosper you and not to harm you, plans to give you hope and a future." - Jeremiah 29:11

Cultivating self-compassion aligns with the message conveyed in the biblical quotation from Jeremiah 29:11: "For I know the plans I have for you, declares the Lord, plans to prosper you and not to harm you, plans to give you hope and a future." This verse highlights the idea that there is a divine plan for each individual, one that is rooted in goodness, hope, and a promising future.

When we approach self-discovery with self-compassion, we acknowledge that we are part of a larger plan, guided by a higher power or purpose. This understanding allows us to view our journey of self-exploration as a process filled with opportunities for growth, healing, and fulfilment. It reminds us that we are not alone in our struggles or challenges and that there is a greater source of love and support available to us.

Treating ourselves with kindness, understanding, and acceptance is an embodiment of the divine love and compassion we receive from a higher power. By extending this compassion to ourselves, we align with the message in Jeremiah 29:11. We recognize that the plans for our lives are meant to prosper us and bring us hope, even when the path may seem uncertain or difficult.

Self-compassion allows us to embrace our strengths, weaknesses, and imperfections as part of our unique journey. It encourages us to approach ourselves with the same love and acceptance that a benevolent Creator extends to us. Through self-compassion, we can navigate the highs and lows of self-discovery with grace and resilience, knowing that we are supported and guided by a divine plan.

self-compassion helps us develop a sense of trust and faith in the future. Just as Jeremiah 29:11 assures us of a promising future, self-compassion reminds us that we are capable of overcoming challenges, learning from our experiences, and creating a fulfilling life aligned with our authentic selves. It strengthens our belief that, despite any setbacks or uncertainties, there is a purposeful path ahead, filled with possibilities and opportunities for growth.

In summary, the biblical quotation from Jeremiah 29:11 emphasizes the divine plans to prosper, provide hope, and shape a promising future. Cultivating self-compassion aligns with this message by fostering kindness, understanding, and acceptance towards ourselves as we embark on the journey of self-discovery. By embracing self-compassion, we can nurture our inner selves, develop resilience, and trust in the greater plan that unfolds before us.

PART THREE

BUILDING A STRONG FOUNDATION OF SELF-LOVE

"Love your neighbour as yourself." - Mark 12:31

In the pursuit of personal growth and fulfilment, one often encounters the timeless wisdom found in religious texts. Among these teachings is a profound verse from the book of Mark in the Bible, which states, "Love your neighbour as yourself" (Mark 12:31). This powerful message underscores the importance of cultivating self-love as a foundation for our interactions with others and our overall well-being.

Building a strong foundation of self-love is a transformative journey that involves developing a deep and unconditional regard for oneself. It goes beyond mere self-esteem or self-confidence, as it encompasses compassion, acceptance, and nurturing care for our well-being. Just as the verse from Mark suggests, loving ourselves serves as the cornerstone for extending love, kindness, and understanding to those around us.

When we embrace self-love, we recognize our inherent worthiness, acknowledging that we are deserving of love and compassion, simply by virtue of being human. This mindset empowers us to prioritize our physical, emotional, and spiritual needs, fostering a greater sense of self-care and well-being. It becomes a conscious choice to treat ourselves with kindness, respect, and forgiveness, embracing our strengths, weaknesses, and imperfections.

To a greater degree, cultivating self-love enables us to form healthier relationships with others. When we truly love ourselves, we become more capable of authentically loving and accepting those around us. This shift in perspective allows us to approach our interactions with empathy, understanding, and compassion. By acknowledging our needs and boundaries, we establish healthier dynamics and foster deeper connections in our relationships.

However, building a strong foundation of self-love is not always easy. Society often encourages self-criticism, comparison, and unrealistic standards that can hinder our journey towards self-acceptance. It requires conscious effort to challenge these societal messages and cultivate self-compassion. It involves embracing our vulnerabilities, practicing self-care, and engaging in introspection to uncover and heal deep-seated wounds.

In this exploration of building a strong foundation of self-love, we will delve into various strategies, practices, and perspectives that can aid us on this transformative journey. From cultivating self-compassion and mindfulness to practicing gratitude and setting healthy boundaries, each step contributes to the nurturing of our inner selves. By anchoring ourselves in self-love, we lay the groundwork for personal growth, meaningful relationships, and a fulfilling life.

As we embark on this exploration, let us remember the profound wisdom contained within the biblical verse from Mark 12:31. By loving ourselves as we love our neighbours, we foster a deep wellspring of love, compassion, and understanding that can positively impact not only our lives but also the lives of those around us.

UNDERSTANDING THE ESSENCE OF SELF-LOVE

Self-love is the foundation upon which personal growth and well-being are built. It encompasses a deep sense of appreciation, acceptance, and compassion for oneself. By recognizing our worthiness and nurturing our well-being, self-love enables us to lead fulfilling and meaningful lives.

Self-love is the practice of treating ourselves with kindness, respect, and understanding. It involves acknowledging and embracing our strengths, weaknesses, and imperfections without judgment. Self-love is rooted in the belief that we are deserving of love and care simply because we exist.

Significance in personal growth: Self-love is essential for personal growth as it provides the necessary nourishment and support for our development. When we love ourselves, we are more inclined to set healthy boundaries, pursue our passions, and take care of our physical, emotional, and spiritual well-being. It empowers us to embrace opportunities, learn from failures, and continuously strive for self-improvement.

Differentiating self-love from self-esteem and self-confidence: While self-esteem and self-confidence are related concepts, they differ from self-love. Self-esteem refers to the evaluation of our worth and capabilities. It can fluctuate based on external validation and achievements. Self-confidence, on the other hand, relates to our belief in our abilities to succeed in specific areas. Both self-esteem and self-confidence can be influenced by external factors. Self-love, however, is an unconditional regard for ourselves, independent of external validation or achievements. It is a holistic and enduring acceptance and care for our whole being.

Connection between self-love and overall well-being: Self-love is intimately tied to overall well-being. When we love ourselves, we prioritize self-care, making choices that nourish our mind, body, and spirit. It promotes a positive self-image, enhances resilience, and fosters emotional well-being. Self-love also influences the quality of our relationships, as it enables us to set healthy boundaries, communicate effectively, and engage in authentic connections. Furthermore, self-love contributes to our ability to navigate challenges, cope with stress, and cultivate a sense of inner peace and fulfilment.

In summary, self-love is the foundation for personal growth and well-being. It involves treating ourselves with kindness, respect, and compassion, independent of external validation or achievements. By practicing self-love, we prioritize self-care, nurture our overall well-being, and develop a positive self-image. It is through self-love that we cultivate resilience, enhance our relationships, and embark on a transformative journey of self-discovery and growth.

CULTIVATING SELF-COMPASSION AND ACCEPTANCE:

Self-compassion and acceptance are fundamental aspects of building a strong foundation of self-love. They involve embracing kindness, understanding, and forgiveness towards oneself, fostering a deep sense of acceptance and appreciation for our strengths, weaknesses, and imperfections.

Embracing self-compassion as a key component of self-love: Self-compassion involves treating ourselves with the same care and understanding that we would extend to a loved one. It encompasses being gentle and supportive towards ourselves during difficult times, acknowledging our pain and suffering without judgment. By practicing self-compassion, we cultivate a sense of warmth and nurturing towards our well-being, recognizing that we are deserving of love and understanding.

Nurturing a non-judgmental and forgiving attitude towards oneself: Self-acceptance requires letting go of self-judgment and cultivating a forgiving attitude towards our mistakes and shortcomings. It involves recognizing that being human entails making errors and experiencing setbacks. Instead of dwelling on self-criticism, we learn to embrace our imperfections as part of our unique journey. Through forgiveness and self-empathy, we release the burden of guilt and create space for growth and self-improvement.

Embracing acceptance of strengths, weaknesses, and imperfections: Accepting ourselves fully means embracing both our strengths and weaknesses. It involves acknowledging and celebrating our accomplishments, talents, and positive attributes, recognizing our inherent worthiness. Simultaneously, self-acceptance entails embracing our vulnerabilities, limitations, and areas for growth. By accepting our imperfections, we foster a sense of authenticity and create room for personal development and self-discovery.

Cultivating self-compassion and acceptance allows us to develop a more compassionate and nurturing relationship with ourselves. It enables us to respond to our pain, challenges, and mistakes with kindness and understanding, rather than harsh self-criticism. By embracing our strengths and weaknesses, we create an environment of self-acceptance, where we can grow and flourish authentically.

PRACTICAL STRATEGIES FOR CULTIVATING SELF-COMPASSION AND ACCEPTANCE INCLUDES

Mindful self-awareness: Developing awareness of our thoughts, emotions, and self-talk helps us identify self-judgment and replace it with self-compassion and acceptance.

Self-reflective practices: Engaging in introspection, journaling, or therapy allows us to explore underlying beliefs and narratives that may hinder self-compassion and acceptance, and work towards reframing them.

Self-care rituals: Engaging in self-care activities that nurture our well-being, such as practicing mindfulness, engaging in hobbies, or spending time in nature, reinforces self-compassion and self-acceptance.

Cultivating a support system: Surrounding ourselves with supportive and understanding individuals who encourage self-compassion and acceptance can provide invaluable emotional support and encouragement.

Practicing self-forgiveness: Acknowledging our mistakes, taking responsibility, and forgiving ourselves allows us to move forward with self-compassion and acceptance.

By cultivating self-compassion and acceptance, we foster a loving and nurturing relationship with ourselves. We embrace our strengths, weaknesses, and imperfections with kindness, understanding, and forgiveness. Through these practices, we create a solid foundation of self-love, empowering us to navigate life's challenges with resilience, authenticity, and a deep sense of inner peace.

PRACTICING SELF-CARE AND PRIORITIZING WELL-BEING

Self-care is a vital aspect of building self-love and maintaining overall well-being. It involves actively attending to our physical, emotional, and spiritual needs, and making deliberate choices that nurture and support our well-being. By understanding the importance of self-care, identifying our personal needs and boundaries, and integrating self-care practices into our daily lives, we can cultivate a strong foundation of self-love and enhance our overall quality of life.

Understanding the importance of self-care in building self-love: Self-care is not a selfish act but rather an essential practice in honouring and nurturing ourselves. It acknowledges that our well-being is important and deserves attention. When we prioritize self-care, we send a powerful message to ourselves that we are deserving of love, respect, and care. It builds a foundation of self-love by demonstrating that our needs matter and should be met.

Identifying and honouring personal needs and boundaries: Each individual has unique needs and boundaries that should be identified and respected. Understanding our physical, emotional, and spiritual needs helps us determine what practices and activities contribute to our well-being. Additionally, establishing and honouring personal boundaries is crucial in maintaining a healthy balance in our lives. It involves recognizing and communicating our limits and ensuring that our needs and values are respected by others.

Exploring various self-care practices and integrating them into daily life: Self-care practices can vary greatly depending on individual preferences, but they all aim to nourish and rejuvenate our mind, body, and spirit. Examples of self-care activities include engaging in regular exercise, practicing mindfulness and meditation, engaging in creative pursuits, spending time in nature, connecting with loved ones, seeking support when needed, and maintaining a healthy work-life balance. Integrating these practices into our daily routines allows us to consistently prioritize self-care and reinforce our commitment to self-love.

Incorporating self-care into our lives requires intention and commitment. Here are some strategies to help integrate self-care practices into daily life:

Create a self-care routine: Designate specific times for self-care activities and make them a non-negotiable part of your schedule.

Start small and build momentum: Begin with small self-care practices that are easily manageable and gradually expand your repertoire as you become more comfortable.

Practice self-awareness: Tune in to your needs

and emotions, and adjust your self-care practices accordingly. Listen to your body and mind, and give yourself what you truly need.

Set boundaries: Learn to say no to commitments or activities that deplete your energy and prioritize those that align with your well-being. Respect your limits and communicate them effectively to others.

Seek support: Reach out to friends, family, or professionals who can provide guidance, accountability, and encouragement on your self-care journey.

Practice self-compassion: Embrace self-compassion when setbacks occur or when self-care practices feel challenging. Be patient and gentle with yourself, knowing that self-care is an ongoing process.

By practicing self-care and prioritizing our well-being, we reinforce the foundation of self-love. We recognize our worthiness and make a conscious choice to prioritize our physical, emotional, and spiritual needs. As a result, we cultivate resilience, reduce stress, enhance our overall well-being, and foster a deep sense of self-love and self-worth.

UNCOVERING AND HEALING DEEP-SEATED

WOUNDS:

Our past experiences can significantly impact our ability to cultivate self-love. Unresolved emotional wounds, traumas, or negative belief systems acquired during childhood or throughout our lives can create barriers to self-love. By exploring the impact of past experiences on self-love, engaging in self-reflection and healing techniques, and seeking professional support, we can begin the journey of uncovering and healing deep-seated wounds.

Exploring the impact of past experiences on self-love: Our experiences, especially those that have been challenging or traumatic, can shape our beliefs about ourselves and our worthiness of love and care. Negative experiences, criticism, or neglect can lead to self-doubt, low self-esteem, and difficulty in practicing self-love. Understanding the connection between past experiences and present self-perception is an essential step in healing and cultivating self-love.

Techniques for self-reflection and healing emotional wounds: Self-reflection is a powerful tool for uncovering and healing deep-seated wounds. Engaging in practices such as journaling, meditation, or therapy can help identify patterns, beliefs, and emotions that contribute to self-limiting beliefs or self-sabotaging behaviours. By examining these wounds and their underlying causes, we can develop a deeper understanding of ourselves and initiate the healing process.

Some techniques for self-reflection and healing includes:

Journaling: Writing about past experiences, emotions, and beliefs can provide insight and help release pent-up emotions.

Meditation and mindfulness: Practicing meditation and mindfulness allows us to observe our thoughts and emotions without judgment, creating space for healing and self-compassion.

Inner child work: Connecting with our inner child and addressing unmet needs or emotional wounds from childhood can facilitate healing and self-love.

Affirmations and positive self-talk: Replacing negative self-talk with affirmations and positive statements can gradually reframe our beliefs and nurture self-love.

Seeking professional support in the healing process: Healing deep-seated wounds often requires support from trained professionals, such as therapists, counsellors, Religious leaders or psychologists. These professionals can provide a safe and supportive environment for exploring past experiences, processing emotions, and implementing effective healing strategies. They can offer guidance, tools, and techniques tailored to individual needs, accelerating the healing journey and facilitating the cultivation of self-love.

It is important to remember that healing is a unique and personal journey, and the process may take time. Be patient and compassionate with yourself as you navigate the process of uncovering and healing deep-seated wounds. By engaging in self-reflection, utilizing healing techniques, and seeking professional support when needed, you can gradually release the emotional burdens of the past, foster self-compassion, and cultivate a deeper sense of self-love.

CULTIVATING MINDFULNESS AND PRESENCE

Mindfulness is a powerful practice that can enhance self-awareness, self-compassion, and overall well-being. By consciously bringing our attention to the present moment without judgment, we can develop a deeper understanding of ourselves, cultivate self-compassion, and navigate challenging emotions and thoughts with greater clarity and resilience. Let's explore the

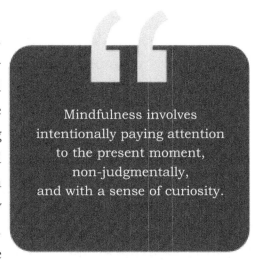

"

Mindfulness involves intentionally paying attention to the present moment, non-judgmentally, and with a sense of curiosity.

role of mindfulness in developing self-awareness and self-compassion, techniques for practicing mindfulness, and how it can help us navigate challenging experiences.

The role of mindfulness in developing self-awareness and self-compassion: Mindfulness involves intentionally paying attention to the present moment, non-judgmentally, and with a sense of curiosity. Through this practice, we can cultivate self-awareness by observing our thoughts, emotions, bodily sensations, and the environment without getting entangled in them. This awareness allows us to recognize patterns, triggers, and automatic reactions that may hinder self-love and compassionate understanding. By observing ourselves with kindness and acceptance, mindfulness promotes self-compassion, as we learn to respond to our experiences with greater understanding and gentleness.

Techniques for practicing mindfulness and staying present in the moment

Mindfulness can be cultivated through various techniques that anchor our attention to the present moment. Here are some practices to consider-

Mindful breathing: Focus your attention on the sensation of the breath, observing each inhalation and exhalation. This technique helps ground you in the present moment and brings awareness to the rhythm of your breath.

Body scan meditation: Direct your attention to different parts of your body, starting from the top of your head and moving down to your toes. Notice any sensations, tension, or areas of relaxation without judgment.

Mindful observation: Engage your senses fully in the present moment by paying attention to the details of your surroundings. Notice colours, shapes, sounds, textures, and smells, allowing yourself to be fully present with what is.

Mindful movement: Engage in activities like yoga, tai chi, or walking meditation, focusing your attention on the sensations and movements of your body. Notice how your body feels and the connection between movement and breath.

Using mindfulness to navigate challenging emotions and thoughts: Mindfulness can be a valuable tool in navigating challenging emotions and thoughts. When difficult emotions arise, instead of suppressing or avoiding them, we can use mindfulness to observe them with curiosity and non-judgmental awareness. By creating space for these emotions, we can gain clarity, understand their underlying causes, and respond to them with self-compassion and understanding. Mindfulness also helps us recognize unhelpful thought patterns and disengage from automatic negative thinking, allowing us to reframe our thoughts and cultivate a more positive and supportive mind-set.

Incorporating mindfulness into daily life requires practice and consistency. Here are some strategies to help integrate mindfulness into your routine:

✓ Set aside dedicated time for formal mindfulness practice, such as meditation or body scan exercises.

- ✓ Integrate mindfulness into daily activities by bringing full attention to the present moment. For example, savour your meals mindfully, engage fully in conversations, or be present while engaging in routine tasks.
- ✓ Use reminders or cues throughout the day to bring your awareness back to the present moment. It could be a chime, a sticky note, or an app that prompts you to pause and be mindful.
- ✓ Find a community or group to support your mindfulness practice, such as joining a meditation group or participating in mindfulness-based programs.

By cultivating mindfulness and presence, we develop a deeper connection with ourselves, foster self-awareness, and nurture self-compassion. Mindfulness enables us to navigate challenging emotions and thoughts with greater clarity and resilience, leading to a more grounded and balanced experience of life. With practice and patience,

PRACTICING GRATITUDE AND CELEBRATING SELF

Gratitude is a transformative practice that can profoundly impact our ability to cultivate self-love and experience greater fulfilment in life. By cultivating gratitude, we shift our focus from what is lacking or negative to appreciating and acknowledging the abundance and blessings in our lives. In this section, we will explore the transformative power of gratitude in building self-love, techniques for cultivating a gratitude practice, and the importance of celebrating our achievements, strengths, and self-growth.

The transformative power of gratitude in building self-love: Gratitude serves as a powerful tool in building self-love by shifting our perspective and focusing on the positive aspects of ourselves and our lives. When we practice gratitude, we acknowledge and appreciate our unique qualities, experiences, and accomplishments. This practice helps us cultivate self-acceptance, self-worth, and a deeper sense of love and compassion towards ourselves. Gratitude also fosters a positive mindset, resilience, and a greater ability to find joy and contentment in the present moment.

Techniques for cultivating a gratitude practice

Cultivating gratitude is a conscious practice that

can be incorporated into our daily lives. Here are some techniques to help cultivate a gratitude practice:

Gratitude journaling: Set aside time each day to write down three to five things you are grateful for. Reflect on the specific reasons why you appreciate them, and allow yourself to truly feel the gratitude in your heart.

Gratitude meditation: During meditation, focus your attention on feelings of gratitude. Bring to mind people, experiences, or aspects of your life that you are grateful for, and let the sensations of gratitude fill your being.

Gratitude rituals: Create simple rituals that remind you to cultivate gratitude. It could be a gratitude jar, where you write down things you are grateful for and place them in the jar. Regularly review the notes to reinforce the positive feelings.

Expressing gratitude to others: Take time to express your gratitude to the people in your life who have had a positive impact on you. Write a heartfelt note, have a sincere conversation, or perform acts of kindness to show your appreciation.

Celebrating achievements, strengths, and self-growth: Celebrating our achievements, strengths, and self-growth is an essential aspect of self-love. By recognizing and acknowledging our accomplishments, we reinforce our self-worth and foster a positive self-image. Celebrating milestones, big or small, encourages self-empowerment and inspires us to continue growing and striving for our goals. It is also important to recognize and embrace our strengths, as they are unique qualities that contribute to our individuality and make us who we are. By celebrating our strengths, we cultivate self-confidence and self-acceptance.

Some ways to celebrate achievements, strengths, and self-growth includes-

Reflection and appreciation: Take time to reflect on your achievements, strengths, and personal growth. Acknowledge the efforts and perseverance that have brought you to where you are today. Appreciate the progress you have made on your journey of self-discovery and self-love.

Reward yourself: Treat yourself to something special as a reward for your accomplishments. It could be a small indulgence, a self-care activity, or an experience that brings you joy.

Share with others: Share your achievements and growth with trusted friends or loved ones who can celebrate with you. Allow their support and encouragement to amplify your sense of accomplishment.

Create a celebration ritual: Develop a personal ritual or ceremony to commemorate significant milestones or moments of self-growth. This could involve lighting a candle, writing a letter to yourself, or engaging in a symbolic gesture that represents your achievements.

By practicing gratitude and celebrating our achievements, strengths, and self-growth, we foster a deeper sense of self

SETTING HEALTHY BOUNDARIES AND HONOURING AUTHENTICITY

Setting and maintaining healthy boundaries is an essential aspect of cultivating self-love and fostering healthy relationships. Boundaries define and protect our personal space, values, needs, and limits, ensuring that we honour ourselves and maintain our well-being. In this section, we will explore the importance of boundaries in self-love and relationships, techniques for setting and communicating personal boundaries effectively, and the significance of embracing authenticity and expressing our true selves without fear of judgment.

Understanding the importance of boundaries in self-love and relationships: Boundaries are vital in establishing and maintaining a healthy sense of self-love. They serve as guidelines that communicate our needs, values, and limits, creating a safe space for self-care, self-respect, and self-expression. Boundaries also play a crucial role in relationships, ensuring mutual respect, trust, and emotional well-being. By setting and honouring boundaries, we protect our physical and emotional energy, establish healthy dynamics, and foster deeper connections based on authenticity and mutual understanding.

Techniques for setting and communicating personal boundaries: Here are some techniques to help you set and communicate personal boundaries effectively-

Self-awareness: Take time to reflect on your needs, values, and limits. Understand what feels comfortable and aligned with your authentic self. This self-awareness forms the foundation for setting clear and meaningful boundaries.

Identify boundaries: Identify areas in your life where you need to establish boundaries. This could include time, personal space, emotional availability, relationships, work, or social commitments. Consider what is acceptable and what crosses your boundaries.

Clear communication: Clearly and assertively communicate your boundaries to others. Use "I" statements to express your needs and expectations, and be specific about the behaviours or actions that are acceptable or not. Practice effective communication skills, such as active listening and expressing empathy, to encourage understanding and respect from others.

Practice self-care: Prioritize self-care as an essential aspect of setting and maintaining boundaries. Take time to recharge, engage in activities that bring you joy and nourish your well-being. This reinforces your commitment to honouring yourself and your boundaries.

EMBRACING AUTHENTICITY AND EXPRESSING TRUE SELF WITHOUT FEAR OF JUDGMENT

Authenticity is the practice of embracing and expressing our true selves, free from the fear of judgment or rejection. It is an integral part of self-love and personal growth. Here are some steps to embrace authenticity-

Self-acceptance: Cultivate self-acceptance by acknowledging and embracing your strengths, weaknesses, and unique qualities. Recognize that you are worthy of love and respect just as you are.

Letting go of perfectionism: Release the need for perfection and embrace your imperfections. Understand that authenticity is about being genuine, not about meeting external expectations or standards.

Overcoming fear of judgment: Recognize that everyone has their own judgments and opinions, but they do not define your worth. Shift your focus from seeking approval to honouring your true self.

Expressing your true self: Take small steps in expressing your authentic self in various aspects of your life. Share your thoughts, feelings, and opinions honestly and respectfully. Engage in activities that align with your passions and values.

Remember that setting boundaries and embracing

authenticity is an ongoing process. It requires self-reflection, self-compassion, and the courage to honour yourself. As you establish healthy boundaries and embrace your true self, you create an empowering environment that supports self-love, personal growth, and meaningful connections with others.

CHALLENGING SOCIETY'S STANDARDS AND EMBRACING INDIVIDUALITY

In our journey of self-love, it is important to recognize and question the societal messages and standards that often hinder our ability to fully embrace ourselves. Society often imposes unrealistic expectations and norms that can negatively impact our self-esteem and self-worth. In this section, we will explore the importance of recognizing and questioning these societal messages, embracing our individuality and self-expression, and overcoming the harmful habit of comparison by embracing our uniqueness.

Recognizing and questioning societal messages that hinder self-love: Society bombards us with messages about how we should look, behave, and live our lives. These messages often perpetuate narrow definitions of beauty, success, and happiness, which can lead to self-doubt, insecurity, and a sense of inadequacy. By becoming aware of these societal messages and questioning their validity, we can free ourselves from their negative influence and make choices that align with our authentic selves. It is crucial to understand that our worth and value as individuals are not defined by external standards but by our inherent qualities, uniqueness, and personal values.

Embracing individuality and self-expression: Each of us is inherently unique, with our personal set of strengths, passions, and perspectives. Embracing our individuality means honouring and celebrating these qualities without seeking validation or conforming to societal expectations. It involves expressing ourselves authentically, whether through our appearance, interests, hobbies, or career choices. Embracing our individuality allows us to tap into our true potential, cultivate self-love, and find fulfilment by living in alignment with our authentic selves.

Overcoming comparison and embracing uniqueness: Comparison is a common habit that can undermine our self-love and hinder our journey of self-discovery. When we constantly compare ourselves to others, we overlook our strengths, achievements, and unique qualities. Overcoming comparison requires cultivating self-compassion and shifting our focus from external comparisons to internal growth. Instead of measuring ourselves against others, we can focus on our personal progress, celebrate our achievements, and appreciate our unique path. Embracing our uniqueness means recognizing that we are not meant to be like anyone else; we are meant to be ourselves, and that is where our true power and beauty lie.

Practices that can help in challenging society's standards and embracing individuality includes-

Self-reflection: Take time for self-reflection to gain clarity on your values, interests, and aspirations. Understand what truly matters to you and what brings you joy and fulfilment.

Surround yourself with positivity: Surround yourself with people, media, and communities that embrace and celebrate individuality. Seek out role models who inspire you to be true to yourself and challenge societal norms.

Practice self-acceptance and self-compassion:
Cultivate self-acceptance by embracing all aspects of yourself, including perceived flaws and imperfections. Treat yourself with kindness, understanding, and forgiveness as you navigate the journey of self-discovery.

Explore self-expression: Engage in activities that allow you to express your authentic self, whether it's through art, writing, music, fashion, or any form of creative self-expression. Allow yourself to explore and experiment without fear of judgment.

Remember, embracing your individuality and challenging society's standards is an ongoing process. It requires courage, self-awareness, and a commitment to living authentically. By embracing your uniqueness and celebrating the qualities that make you who you are, you can cultivate a deep sense of self-love and live a more fulfilling and meaningful life.

FOSTERING LOVING RELATIONSHIPS AND CONNECTIONS

Building and nurturing loving relationships and connections is an integral part of our journey of self-love. The relationships we cultivate can either support and enhance our self-love or hinder our growth. In this section, we will examine the connection between self-love and healthy relationships, explore ways to nurture supportive and loving connections in our lives, and discuss the importance of surrounding ourselves with people who uplift and affirm our self-love.

Examining the connection between self-love and healthy relationships: Self-love lays the foundation for healthy and fulfilling relationships. When we love ourselves, we establish a strong sense of self-worth, self-acceptance, and self-respect. This allows us to set and maintain healthy boundaries, communicate our needs effectively, and make choices that align with our values and well-being. Self-love also enables us to show up authentically and vulnerably in relationships, fostering deeper connections and intimacy.

Nurturing supportive and loving connections in one's life: To foster loving relationships, it is important to nurture connections that align with our self-love journey. Here are some ways to cultivate supportive and loving connections:

Authenticity and vulnerability: Be authentic and vulnerable in your relationships, allowing yourself to be seen and understood. Share your thoughts, feelings, and experiences openly, and encourage others to do the same. This creates an environment of trust and deepens the connection.

Communication and active listening: Practice open and honest communication in your relationships. Listen actively to others, seeking to understand their perspectives and experiences without judgment. Engage in compassionate and nonviolent communication to resolve conflicts and maintain healthy dynamics.

Mutual respect and support: Cultivate relationships based on mutual respect, where both parties value and support each other's growth, dreams, and well-being. Offer encouragement, empathy, and assistance when needed, and celebrate each other's successes and milestones.

Healthy boundaries: Establish and maintain healthy boundaries in your relationships. Communicate your needs, limits, and expectations clearly, and respect the boundaries of others. Healthy boundaries create a space for mutual respect and understanding.

Surrounding oneself with people who uplift and

affirm self-love: The people we surround ourselves with can greatly impact our self-love journey. It is important to seek out and maintain relationships with individuals who uplift and affirm our self-love. Surround yourself with people who appreciate and celebrate your uniqueness, support your growth, and inspire you to love yourself more deeply. Distance yourself from toxic relationships or individuals who undermine your self-worth and drain your energy.

Remember that fostering loving relationships and connections is a two-way process. It requires effort, open communication, and a willingness to cultivate and nurture meaningful connections. By surrounding yourself with people who uplift and affirm your self-love, you create a supportive network that encourages your personal growth, well-being, and continued journey of self-discovery and self-love.

SUSTAINING AND GROWING SELF-LOVE

Self-love is not a destination but an ongoing journey of growth and evolution. It requires continuous nurturing and care, especially in the face of challenges and setbacks. In this section, we will explore strategies for maintaining self-love, embracing it as a lifelong journey, and finding inspiration and support along the way.

Strategies for maintaining self-love in the face of challenges: Life is filled with ups and downs, and maintaining self-love during challenging times is crucial. Here are some strategies to help you sustain self-love:

Self-compassion: Practice self-compassion by treating yourself with kindness, understanding, and acceptance during difficult moments. Be gentle with yourself, acknowledge your emotions, and offer yourself words of encouragement and support.

Self-care: Prioritize self-care as a regular practice to recharge and nourish yourself. Engage in activities that bring you joy, relaxation, and rejuvenation. This can include hobbies, exercise, spending time in nature, practicing mindfulness, or seeking professional help when needed.

Positive self-talk: Monitor your inner dialogue and replace self-criticism with self-affirmation. Challenge negative self-talk and replace it with positive and empowering statements. Remind yourself of your strengths, accomplishments, and qualities that make you unique.

Seek support: Reach out to trusted friends, family members, or support groups who can provide a listening ear, encouragement, and guidance. Surrounding yourself with a supportive network helps you feel validated, understood, and uplifted during challenging times.

Embracing self-love as an ongoing journey of growth and evolution: Self-love is not a destination to be reached but an ongoing process of growth and evolution. Embrace the idea that self-love is a lifelong journey filled with ups and downs, triumphs and setbacks, and continuous self-discovery. Allow yourself to evolve, learn, and adapt along the way, knowing that self-love is a dynamic and ever-changing experience.

View challenges as opportunities for growth and self-reflection. Each obstacle or setback can provide valuable lessons and insights about yourself, your values, and your resilience. Embrace the process of self-discovery and personal growth, knowing that self-love is not about being perfect but about accepting and loving yourself unconditionally, flaws and all.

Finding inspiration and support in the process: Surround yourself with inspiration and sources of support that reinforce your self-love journey. Seek out books, podcasts, or workshops that promote self-love, personal growth, and empowerment. Engage in activities that uplift and inspire you, such as journaling, affirmations, or visualization exercises.

Additionally, connect with individuals who have embarked on similar journeys or who embody self-love and personal growth. Seek out mentors, role models, or communities that can provide guidance, inspiration, and encouragement along the way.

Remember that sustaining and growing self-love requires consistent effort and commitment. Be patient and kind to yourself as you navigate the ups and downs of the journey. Celebrate your progress, no matter how small, and embrace the continuous evolution of self-love as an empowering and transformative process.

PART FOUR

CULTIVATING MEANINGFUL RELATIONSHIPS

"Two are better than one because they have a good return for their labour." - Ecclesiastes 4:9

The power of human connection and the importance of meaningful relationships have been acknowledged for centuries. As the biblical verse from Ecclesiastes 4:9 reminds us, "Two are better than one because they have a good return for their labour." Our relationships not only enhance our lives but also have the potential to contribute to our personal growth, happiness, and overall well-being.

In this part, we will explore the significance of cultivating meaningful relationships, both in our personal lives and in our broader communities. We will delve into the various dimensions of these relationships, such as friendships, romantic partnerships, family bonds, and connections with our communities. Through examining the benefits, challenges, and strategies for nurturing meaningful relationships, we can develop a deeper understanding of the impact they have on our lives. Meaningful relationships go beyond surface-level interactions and are characterized by mutual respect, trust, support, and shared experiences. They provide us with a sense of belonging, intimacy, and emotional support during both the joyful and challenging moments of life. By investing

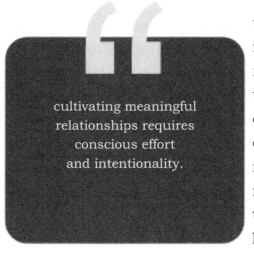

cultivating meaningful relationships requires conscious effort and intentionality.

time and effort into building and maintaining these connections, we can create a network of relationships that enriches our lives and contributes to our personal and spiritual growth.

However, cultivating meaningful relationships requires conscious effort and intentionality. It involves developing effective communication skills, practicing empathy and compassion, and being willing to invest time and energy in nurturing the connections we value. It also requires recognizing and appreciating the unique qualities and perspectives that each individual brings to the relationship, fostering an environment of mutual growth and understanding.

Furthermore, meaningful relationships extend beyond our immediate circles to encompass our communities and the wider world. Engaging with and contributing to our communities allows us to form connections with people who share common interests, values, and goals. Through acts of service, collaboration, and active participation, we can build bridges and create a positive impact on the lives of others, fostering a sense of interconnectedness and purpose.

In the following sections, we will delve into the various aspects of cultivating meaningful relationships. We will explore topics such as effective communication, conflict resolution, building trust, maintaining healthy boundaries, and nurturing relationships with ourselves and others. By gaining insights and practical strategies in these areas, we can develop and sustain relationships that bring joy, fulfilment, and personal growth.

So let us embark on this journey of cultivating meaningful relationships, recognizing the wisdom in Ecclesiastes that affirms the value of companionship and the rewards that come from the labour we invest in fostering connections with others. Together, we can learn, grow, and create a world where meaningful relationships flourish, bringing happiness, support, and a sense of purpose to our lives.

THE POWER OF CONNECTION

Exploring the Significance of Human Connection and Its Impact on Our Well-being

Human beings are inherently social creatures. We have an innate need for connection and belonging. From the earliest moments of our lives, we seek bonds with others, forming relationships that shape our experiences and influence our well-being. The biblical verse from Ecclesiastes 4:9 reminds us of the inherent value of connection, stating that "two are better than one because they have a good return for their labour." In this section, we will delve into the significance of human connection and its profound impact on our well-being.

Understanding the Essence of Connection:

Connection encompasses more than just superficial interactions. It involves the experience of being seen, heard, and understood by others. It is the foundation upon which relationships are built and nurtured. Connection provides us with a sense of belonging, purpose, and support, and it plays a vital role in our physical, emotional, and mental well-being.

The Impact of Connection on Well-being:

Meaningful connections have a profound impact on our well-being across various dimensions of our lives. Here are some ways in which connection influences our overall well-being.

- ✓ **Emotional well-being:** Meaningful connections provide us with emotional support, empathy, and understanding. They create a safe space for expressing our feelings, sharing our joys and sorrows, and experiencing validation and comfort during challenging times.

- ✓ **Mental well-being:** Connection helps alleviate feelings of loneliness, isolation, and anxiety. It promotes a sense of belonging and fosters a positive mindset, contributing to our mental resilience and overall psychological health.

- ✓ **Physical well-being:** Research shows that social connection can have a significant impact on our physical health. Strong social support systems are associated with lower rates of stress, improved immune function, and even increased longevity.

✓ **Self-esteem and self-worth:** Meaningful connections can enhance our self-esteem and self-worth. When we feel seen, appreciated, and valued by others, it reinforces our sense of identity and contributes to a positive self-perception.

CULTIVATING MEANINGFUL CONNECTIONS

Cultivating meaningful connections requires intention, effort, and vulnerability. Here are some strategies for fostering and nurturing these connections-

Active listening: Engage in active listening when interacting with others. Give your full attention, demonstrate empathy, and seek to understand their perspectives and experiences.

Authenticity and vulnerability: Foster deeper connections by being authentic and vulnerable. Share your thoughts, feelings, and experiences openly, allowing others to do the same. This creates an environment of trust and encourages genuine connection.

Cultivating empathy and compassion: Practice empathy and compassion in your interactions. Seek to understand and validate the feelings and experiences of others, demonstrating care and support.

Shared experiences: Engage in activities and experiences that promote shared interests and values. Participating in shared activities can deepen connections and create lasting memories.

Maintaining a balance: Strive for a balance between giving and receiving in relationships. Be willing to offer support and be receptive to receiving support from others, creating a reciprocal exchange of care and connection.

The power of human connection is undeniable. Meaningful connections have a profound impact on our well-being, contributing to our emotional, mental, and physical health. As we embrace the wisdom of Ecclesiastes, let us recognize the significance of connection in our lives. By nurturing and cultivating meaningful connections, we can experience a greater sense of fulfilment, support, and joy, enhancing our overall well-being and enriching the journey of life.

BUILDING TRUST AND VULNERABILITY

Strategies for Developing Trust and Fostering Vulnerability in Relationships

Trust and vulnerability are the cornerstones of deep and meaningful relationships. Trust creates a sense of safety and security, while vulnerability allows for authentic connection and emotional intimacy. Together, they form a solid foundation for nurturing and strengthening relationships. In this section, we will explore strategies for developing trust and fostering vulnerability in relationships, enabling us to build stronger and more fulfilling connections with others.

Understanding Trust and Vulnerability

Trust is the belief in the reliability, honesty, and integrity of another person. It is developed over time through consistent actions, open communication, and reliability. Vulnerability, on the other hand, involves opening ourselves up emotionally, sharing our fears, insecurities, and deepest feelings. It requires a willingness to be seen and heard, even when it feels uncomfortable or uncertain.

STRATEGIES FOR BUILDING TRUST

Consistency and Reliability: Demonstrate consistency and reliability in your words and actions. Follow through on commitments, be dependable, and act with integrity. Consistency over time builds a foundation of trust.

Open Communication: Foster open and honest communication in your relationships. Encourage dialogue, active listening, and expressing thoughts and feelings without judgment. Create a safe space for others to share and be heard.

Trust-Building Activities: Engage in trust-building activities and experiences together. This can include collaborative projects, shared adventures, or working through challenges as a team. These shared experiences can strengthen the bond and foster trust.

Accountability and Transparency: Take responsibility for your actions and be transparent in your intentions. Apologize and make amends when necessary. Being accountable and transparent builds trust and shows a commitment to the relationship.

STRATEGIES FOR FOSTERING VULNERABILITY

Lead by Example: Be willing to be vulnerable first. Share your thoughts, feelings, and experiences authentically and openly. By demonstrating vulnerability, you create a safe space for others to do the same.

Active Listening and Empathy: Practice active listening and empathy when others express their vulnerability. Create a non-judgmental and supportive environment where they feel heard, understood, and accepted.

Validate and Validate: Validate the emotions and experiences shared by others. Offer reassurance, understanding, and empathy, letting them know that their vulnerability is valued and respected.

Gradual Progression: Allow vulnerability to develop gradually in a relationship. Start with smaller, less intimate disclosures and gradually build towards deeper levels of vulnerability. Respect the pace at which others are comfortable sharing and honour their boundaries.

Building trust and fostering vulnerability in relationships are essential for creating deep and meaningful connections. By implementing these strategies, we can cultivate an environment of trust, openness, and authenticity. Remember that building trust and fostering vulnerability is a journey that requires patience, consistency, and mutual support. As we embrace these practices, we can create relationships that are grounded in trust, vulnerability, and emotional intimacy, leading to greater fulfilment and closeness with others.

EFFECTIVE COMMUNICATION
Techniques for Enhancing Communication Skills to Strengthen Relationships

Communication is the lifeblood of relationships. It is the foundation upon which understanding, connection, and mutual growth are built. Effective communication involves both speaking and listening with intention, clarity, and empathy. By honing our communication skills, we can strengthen our relationships and foster a deeper level of understanding and connection with others. In this section, we will explore techniques for enhancing communication skills to cultivate healthier and more meaningful relationships.

Active Listening:

Active listening is a fundamental aspect of effective communication. It involves giving your full attention to the speaker and seeking to understand their perspective and feelings. Key techniques for active listening include:

✓ Maintaining eye contact and open body

language.

- ✓ Avoiding interruptions and allowing the speaker to express themselves fully.
- ✓ Reflecting and paraphrasing to ensure accurate understanding.
- ✓ Asking clarifying questions to gain further insight.

Assertive Communication:

Assertive communication involves expressing your thoughts, feelings, and needs in a clear, honest, and respectful manner. It allows you to communicate your boundaries, desires, and concerns effectively while respecting the rights and perspectives of others. Key techniques for assertive communication include:

- ✓ Using "I" statements to express thoughts and feelings without blaming or attacking.
- ✓ Being clear and specific in your communication, avoiding vague or ambiguous language.
- ✓ Practicing active listening and empathy to understand the perspectives of others.
- ✓ Maintaining a calm and composed demeanour, even in challenging situations.

Non-Verbal Communication:

Non-verbal cues play a significant role in communication. They include facial expressions, body language, tone of voice, and gestures. Being aware of and utilizing non-verbal cues effectively can enhance the clarity and impact of your communication. Key techniques for non-verbal communication include:

- ✓ Maintaining appropriate eye contact to show interest and attentiveness.
- ✓ Using open and relaxed body language to convey openness and receptiveness.
- ✓ Matching your tone of voice with the intended message, emphasizing emotions when necessary.
- ✓ Being mindful of cultural differences in non-verbal communication.

Emotional Intelligence:

Emotional intelligence is the ability to recognize and understand your emotions and the emotions of others. It enables you to respond to emotions in a constructive and empathetic manner. Key techniques for developing emotional intelligence include:

- ✓ Practicing self-awareness and self-reflection to understand your emotions and triggers.

✓ Cultivating empathy to understand the emotions and perspectives of others.

✓ Regulating your emotions and managing emotional reactions during conversations.

✓ Responding with empathy and understanding rather than reacting impulsively.

Effective communication is a vital skill for building and maintaining strong relationships. By actively listening, practicing assertive communication, utilizing non-verbal cues, and developing emotional intelligence, we can enhance our ability to connect, understand, and empathize with others. Remember that effective communication is a continuous process that requires practice, patience, and a willingness to learn and grow. As we integrate these techniques into our interactions, we can foster healthier and more meaningful relationships, leading to greater understanding, trust, and mutual support.

NURTURING FRIENDSHIP

Exploring the Qualities and Practices that Contribute to Deep and Lasting Friendships

Friendship is a cherished bond that brings joy,

support, and companionship into our lives. Deep and lasting friendships have the power to uplift us, provide a sense of belonging, and enrich our overall well-being. In this section, we will delve into the qualities and practices that contribute to the development and nurturing of deep and lasting friendships, allowing us to cultivate meaningful connections that stand the test of time.

Trust and Loyalty

Trust and loyalty are the bedrock of any strong friendship. Being reliable, honest, and trustworthy establishes a foundation of trust, allowing friends to confide in each other and feel secure in their bond. Loyalty entails being there for one another, supporting each other through both triumphs and challenges.

Authenticity and Acceptance

Authenticity is the willingness to show up as your true self, without fear of judgment or preteens. In deep friendships, authenticity fosters a sense of acceptance, as friends appreciate and embrace each other's strengths, quirks, and imperfections. Being able to be vulnerable and genuine with one another creates a safe space for open and honest communication.

Effective Communication

Effective communication is essential in nurturing friendships. It involves active listening, expressing oneself clearly, and being receptive to the thoughts and feelings of your friends. Communicating openly and honestly allows for understanding, resolution of conflicts, and the deepening of emotional connection.

Empathy and Support

Empathy is the ability to understand and share the feelings of others. In deep friendships, empathy allows friends to offer support, compassion, and a listening ear during challenging times. Being there for each other, both in celebration and in moments of struggle, strengthens the bond and fosters a sense of emotional support.

Shared Interests and Memories

Shared interests and experiences create a sense of connection and provide opportunities for meaningful engagement. Engaging in activities together, pursuing common hobbies, and creating lasting memories fosters a sense of camaraderie and strengthens the friendship over time.

Respect and Boundaries

Respect is crucial in any friendship. It involves honouring each other's boundaries, opinions, and decisions. Respecting the individuality and autonomy of your friends contributes to a healthy and balanced dynamic, where everyone feels valued and understood.

Invest Time and Effort

Nurturing deep and lasting friendships requires intentional investment of time and effort. Regularly connecting, whether through face-to-face interactions, phone calls, or virtual communication, helps maintain the bond and shows your friends that they are a priority in your life. Being present and engaged in the friendship demonstrates your commitment to its growth and longevity.

Deep and lasting friendships enrich our lives, providing us with companionship, support, and shared experiences. By embodying qualities such as trust, authenticity, effective communication, empathy, and respect, we can cultivate and nurture these friendships. It is through investing time, effort, and genuine care that we create connections that endure the tests of time. As we prioritize and cultivate these qualities and practices in our friendships, we can experience the beauty and fulfilment that come with deep and lasting connections.

CULTIVATING INTIMACY IN ROMANTIC RELATIONSHIPS

Understanding the Importance of Intimacy and Emotional Connection in Romantic Partnerships

Romantic relationships hold the potential for profound emotional connection, vulnerability, and intimacy. Intimacy goes beyond physical attraction and encompasses a deep emotional bond that fosters trust, understanding, and mutual growth. In this section, we will explore the importance of intimacy and emotional connection in romantic partnerships and delve into strategies for cultivating and nourishing these vital aspects of a healthy and fulfilling relationship.

Emotional Vulnerability

Emotional vulnerability is the foundation of intimacy in romantic relationships. It involves the willingness to open up and share one's authentic thoughts, feelings, and fears. Being vulnerable creates a safe space for both partners to be seen, heard, and understood on a deep emotional level.

Effective Communication

Open and honest communication is a cornerstone of intimacy. It involves actively listening, expressing oneself honestly and respectfully, and being receptive to the needs and emotions of your partner. Through effective communication, couples can build trust, resolve conflicts, and deepen their emotional connection.

Building Trust

Trust is essential for intimacy to thrive in romantic relationships. Trust is developed through consistent actions, transparency, and reliability. Honouring commitments, being truthful, and maintaining confidentiality builds a strong foundation of trust that allows partners to feel safe and secure in their emotional vulnerability.

Cultivating Empathy and Understanding

Empathy and understanding are crucial for fostering emotional connection. Being able to step into your partner's shoes, validate their feelings, and offer support and understanding creates a sense of emotional closeness and deepens the bond between partners. Seeking to understand your partner's perspective and demonstrating empathy strengthens the emotional connection.

Quality Time and Shared Experiences

Spending quality time together and sharing meaningful experiences is vital for fostering intimacy in romantic relationships. Engaging in activities that both partners enjoy, creating new memories, and making time for regular connection deepens the emotional connection and strengthens the bond.

Physical Intimacy

Physical intimacy, including affectionate touch, cuddling, and sexual intimacy, plays a significant role in romantic relationships. Physical touch can express love, comfort, and closeness, fostering a sense of emotional connection and enhancing the overall intimacy in the relationship. It is essential for partners to communicate their needs and desires openly and respectfully in this area.

Continuous Growth and Mutual Support

Cultivating intimacy requires a commitment to continuous growth and mutual support. Encouraging each other's personal growth, offering support during challenging times, and celebrating each other's achievements fosters a sense of partnership and emotional closeness.

Intimacy and emotional connection are vital elements of a healthy and fulfilling romantic relationship. By fostering emotional vulnerability, practicing effective communication, building trust, cultivating empathy, spending quality time together, embracing physical intimacy, and supporting each other's growth, couples can nurture and deepen the intimacy in their relationship. Remember that cultivating intimacy is an ongoing process that requires effort, understanding, and a commitment to emotional connection. As partners prioritize and invest in these aspects of their relationship, they can experience the depth and fulfilment that come with a truly intimate and connected romantic partnership.

STRENGTHENING FAMILY BONDS

Strategies for Nurturing Healthy and Loving Relationships Within the Family Unit

Family is the cornerstone of our lives, providing love, support, and a sense of belonging. Nurturing healthy and loving relationships within the family unit is crucial for the well-being and happiness of all family members. In this section, we will explore strategies for strengthening family bonds, fostering open communication, and cultivating a supportive and harmonious family environment.

Open and Honest Communication

Open and honest communication is essential for building strong family bonds. Encouraging family members to express their thoughts, feelings, and concerns in a safe and non-judgmental environment fosters trust, understanding, and emotional connection. Active listening, empathy, and effective communication techniques, such as using "I" statements and avoiding blame or criticism, promote healthy dialogue within the family.

Quality Time and Shared Activities

Spending quality time together and engaging in shared activities strengthens family bonds. Regularly setting aside dedicated time for family activities, such as family dinners, game nights, outings, or vacations, allows for meaningful connections and creates lasting memories. These shared experiences foster a sense of togetherness, unity, and enjoyment within the family unit.

Mutual Respect and Empathy

Mutual respect and empathy are the building blocks of healthy family relationships. Respecting each family member's individuality, opinions, and boundaries creates a supportive and inclusive environment. Cultivating empathy by seeking to understand and validate each other's experiences and emotions enhances the emotional connection and strengthens family bonds.

Conflict Resolution and Forgiveness

Conflict is inevitable in any family, but how conflicts are resolved greatly impacts the strength of family bonds. Encouraging open and constructive communication during conflicts, actively listening to different perspectives, and finding compromises or solutions that honour everyone's needs promote harmony within the family. Additionally, practicing forgiveness and letting go of grudges or past hurts allows for healing and the restoration of trust and love.

Support and Celebration

Supporting and celebrating each other's achievements, milestones, and personal growth within the family fosters a sense of appreciation and validation. Showing genuine interest, offering encouragement, and being present during both challenging and joyous moments create a strong support system within the family. Celebrating each other's successes and milestones reinforces a culture of love, positivity, and mutual support.

Establishing and Respecting Boundaries

Respecting individual boundaries is crucial for maintaining healthy family relationships. Each family member should have the freedom to express their needs and establish personal boundaries, which should be acknowledged and respected by others. Honouring boundaries promotes mutual respect, emotional safety, and an atmosphere of trust within the family.

Continuous Growth and Adaptation

Families are dynamic and evolve over time. Embracing continuous growth and adaptation allows the family unit to navigate changes and challenges together. Encouraging individual and collective growth, supporting each other's aspirations, and adapting to new circumstances as a family help in maintaining strong and resilient family bonds.

Nurturing healthy and loving relationships within the family unit requires ongoing effort, understanding, and a commitment to open communication, mutual respect, and support. By fostering open and honest communication, spending quality time together, practicing empathy and forgiveness, establishing and respecting boundaries, and embracing continuous growth and adaptation, families can strengthen their bonds and create a loving and harmonious environment. Remember that strong family bonds are built on a foundation of love, acceptance, and shared experiences, and they provide a source of support and happiness for all family members.

EMBRACING DIVERSITY AND INCLUSION

Fostering Meaningful Connections Across Different Cultures, Backgrounds, and Perspectives

In our increasingly interconnected world, embracing diversity and inclusion is essential for building strong and harmonious communities. Fostering meaningful connections across different cultures, backgrounds, and perspectives not only enriches our lives but also promotes understanding, empathy, and a sense of unity. In this section, we will explore strategies for embracing diversity and inclusion, celebrating cultural differences, and fostering connections that bridge divides and promote mutual respect and appreciation.

Cultivating an Open Mindset

Embracing diversity begins with cultivating an open mindset. Being willing to explore and learn about different cultures, beliefs, and perspectives allows for greater understanding and appreciation of our shared humanity. It involves recognizing and challenging our biases and assumptions, and actively seeking to broaden our horizons through education, exposure, and dialogue.

Active Listening and Empathy

Active listening and empathy are essential tools for fostering connections across diverse backgrounds. Actively listening to others' stories, experiences, and perspectives with an open heart and seeking to understand their unique challenges, triumphs, and aspirations helps build bridges of empathy and connection. Cultivating empathy allows us to step into someone else's shoes and appreciate the richness of their experiences.

Celebrating Cultural Differences

Rather than seeing differences as barriers,

celebrating and honouring cultural diversity promotes inclusivity and fosters connections. Organizing cultural events, sharing traditions and customs, and participating in multicultural activities create opportunities for people from different backgrounds to come together, learn from one another, and celebrate the beauty of diversity.

Building Bridges through Dialogue

Open and respectful dialogue serves as a bridge between diverse cultures, backgrounds, and perspectives. Creating safe spaces for conversations, where individuals can express their views without fear of judgment, allows for the exchange of ideas, experiences, and values. Meaningful dialogue promotes understanding, challenges stereotypes, and fosters a sense of connection and shared humanity.

Collaborative Projects and Partnerships

Collaborative projects and partnerships that bring together individuals from diverse backgrounds can create opportunities for meaningful connections. Working together towards a common goal encourages cooperation, understanding, and mutual respect. By leveraging each person's unique strengths and perspectives, collaborative initiatives contribute to a more inclusive and united community.

Education and Awareness

Education and awareness play a vital role in embracing diversity and fostering meaningful connections. Promoting diversity and inclusion through educational programs, workshops, and awareness campaigns helps challenge biases, dismantle stereotypes, and foster a culture of respect and acceptance. By fostering a climate of continuous learning and growth, we can create a more inclusive and understanding society.

Creating Inclusive Spaces

Creating inclusive spaces and environments is crucial for fostering connections across diverse backgrounds. It involves ensuring equal opportunities, promoting diversity in leadership positions, and fostering a culture of respect and inclusivity in schools, workplaces, and community settings. Inclusive spaces allow individuals to bring their whole selves, feel valued, and contribute to the collective well-being.

Embracing diversity and inclusion is an ongoing journey that requires intentional effort and a commitment to building meaningful connections across cultures, backgrounds, and perspectives. By cultivating an open mindset, practicing active listening and empathy, celebrating cultural differences, engaging in dialogue, fostering collaborations, promoting education and awareness, and creating inclusive spaces, we can create a society that values and embraces the richness of diversity. Through these efforts, we foster a sense of belonging, strengthen connections, and work towards a more united and harmonious world.

RESOLVING CONFLICT AND BUILDING RESILIENCE

Techniques for Navigating Conflicts and Challenges in Relationships and Developing Resilience

Conflict is an inevitable part of any relationship, whether it be with family, friends, colleagues, or romantic partners. Navigating conflicts and challenges requires effective communication, empathy, and a commitment to finding mutually satisfactory resolutions. Additionally, developing resilience is essential for bouncing back from difficult situations and maintaining healthy relationships. In this section, we will explore techniques for resolving conflict, fostering resilience, and building stronger connections in the face of challenges.

Active Listening and Empathy

Active listening and empathy are foundational in resolving conflicts. Taking the time to genuinely understand the perspectives and feelings of others promotes open dialogue and a sense of validation. By actively listening and empathizing with each other's experiences, we can foster mutual understanding and find common ground for resolving conflicts.

Effective Communication

Effective communication is crucial for resolving conflicts in a constructive manner. It involves expressing thoughts and feelings clearly and respectfully, using "I" statements to avoid blame, and actively seeking to understand the other person's point of view. Good communication also includes nonverbal cues, such as maintaining eye contact and open body language, to convey attentiveness and receptiveness.

Finding Common Ground and Compromise

In conflicts, it is important to identify areas of common ground and work towards finding compromises that meet the needs of all parties involved. This requires a willingness to let go of rigid positions and explore creative solutions that honour each person's perspective. By focusing on shared goals and seeking win-win outcomes, conflicts can be resolved in a way that strengthens relationships.

Managing Emotions and Conflict Resolution Styles

Understanding and managing emotions play a significant role in conflict resolution. Emotional intelligence allows individuals to recognize and regulate their own emotions, as well as empathize with the emotions of others. Different conflict resolution styles, such as collaborating, compromising, accommodating, or avoiding, can be employed based on the specific situation and desired outcomes.

Practicing Forgiveness and Letting Go

Forgiveness is a powerful tool for resolving conflicts and building resilience in relationships. It involves letting go of resentment, grudges, and past hurts. Forgiveness does not mean condoning harmful behaviour, but rather freeing oneself from the emotional burden that conflict can bring. By practicing forgiveness, individuals can move forward and rebuild trust in relationships.

Building Resilience

Resilience is the ability to bounce back from adversity and maintain emotional well-being. Developing resilience involves cultivating a positive mindset, building a support network, practicing self-care, and learning from challenging experiences. By strengthening our resilience, we can better navigate conflicts and challenges, and grow stronger both individually and in our relationships.

Seeking Mediation or Professional Support

In some cases, conflicts may require external assistance to reach a resolution. Seeking mediation from a neutral third party, such as a trusted friend, family member, or professional mediator, can provide guidance and facilitate productive dialogue. In more complex or deeply rooted conflicts, seeking the support of therapists or counsellors can help individuals navigate the underlying issues and develop healthier relationship dynamics.

Resolving conflicts and building resilience are integral to maintaining healthy and fulfilling relationships. By practicing active listening, effective communication, empathy, and finding common ground, conflicts can be transformed into opportunities for growth and understanding. Cultivating forgiveness, resilience, and seeking external support when needed contribute to the overall strength and well-being of relationships. With these techniques, we can navigate conflicts with grace and develop the resilience necessary to overcome challenges and foster stronger, more fulfilling connections with others.

HEALTHY BOUNDARIES

Establishing and Maintaining Healthy Boundaries to Foster Respect and Maintain Well-being in Relationships

Establishing and maintaining healthy boundaries is crucial for fostering respect, preserving individual well-being, and maintaining healthy relationships. Boundaries serve as guidelines for how we want to be treated, what we are comfortable with, and what is acceptable to us in our interactions with others. In this section, we will explore the importance of healthy boundaries in relationships, techniques for setting and communicating boundaries, and strategies for maintaining them to promote overall well-being.

Understanding Healthy Boundaries

Healthy boundaries are the limits and guidelines we set for ourselves in relationships. They define what is acceptable and respectful behaviour, and they help protect our physical, emotional, and mental well-being. Understanding the importance of healthy boundaries allows us to establish a sense of self-respect and communicate our needs and limits effectively.

Recognizing Personal Needs and Limits

Establishing healthy boundaries begins with self-awareness. It is important to recognize our personal needs, values, and limits. Taking the time to reflect on what makes us comfortable and what feels like a violation of our boundaries empowers us to clearly define and communicate them to others.

Communicating Boundaries Assertively

Assertive communication is key to effectively communicate our boundaries to others. It involves expressing our needs, desires, and limits in a respectful and clear manner. Using "I" statements, expressing our feelings and expectations, and setting consequences for boundary violations can help establish and reinforce our boundaries in relationships.

Respecting Others' Boundaries

Establishing healthy boundaries is a two-way street. Just as we expect others to respect our boundaries, it is essential that we also respect the boundaries of others. Respecting others' boundaries creates an environment of mutual respect, trust, and understanding in relationships.

Adjusting Boundaries as Needed

Boundaries are not fixed and may need adjustment as relationships evolve. It is important to regularly assess and reassess our boundaries to ensure they align with our current needs and values. Adjusting boundaries when necessary allows for growth, change, and the maintenance of healthy relationships.

Self-Care and Boundary Maintenance

Maintaining healthy boundaries requires self-care. Taking care of our physical, emotional, and mental well-being allows us to establish and maintain boundaries that promote our overall health. Prioritizing self-care activities, setting aside personal time, and practicing self-compassion support our ability to uphold healthy boundaries in relationships.

Seeking Support

Sometimes, maintaining healthy boundaries can be challenging, especially when faced with resistance or difficult dynamics in relationships. Seeking support from trusted friends, family members, or professionals can provide guidance, validation, and strategies for navigating boundary-related challenges.

Establishing and maintaining healthy boundaries is crucial for fostering respect, promoting well-being, and maintaining healthy relationships. By understanding our personal needs and limits, communicating assertively, respecting the boundaries of others, adjusting boundaries as needed, practicing self-care, and seeking support when necessary, we can establish a foundation of healthy boundaries that contribute to fulfilling and mutually respectful relationships. By valuing and upholding our boundaries, we cultivate an environment that fosters respect, understanding, and overall well-being for ourselves and those around us.

SELF-LOVE AND RELATIONSHIPS

Exploring the Interplay between Self-Love and Cultivating Meaningful Connections with Others

The journey of self-love and cultivating meaningful relationships are deeply intertwined. When we develop a strong foundation of self-love, it positively impacts our ability to form and sustain healthy connections with others. In this section, we will explore the interplay between self-love and relationships, highlighting how nurturing self-love enhances our capacity to engage in authentic, fulfilling, and supportive connections with others.

Building a Foundation of Self-Love

Self-love forms the basis for all our relationships. It involves developing a deep appreciation and acceptance of ourselves, embracing our strengths and weaknesses, and recognizing our inherent worthiness. By nurturing self-love, we cultivate a sense of inner wholeness and security, which positively influences our interactions with others.

Authenticity and Vulnerability

Self-love empowers us to show up authentically in relationships. When we love ourselves, we can embrace our true selves without fear of judgment or rejection. This authenticity allows for genuine connections, as others can sense our openness and vulnerability. By embracing our authenticity, we create a space for deeper understanding, trust, and intimacy in our relationships.

Boundaries and Respect

Self-love involves setting and maintaining healthy boundaries, which are essential for fostering respect in relationships. When we love ourselves, we recognize our needs, values, and limits, and communicate them effectively to others. By establishing and enforcing boundaries, we create an environment that promotes mutual respect and supports the growth of healthy relationships.

Communication and Emotional Well-being

Self-love enhances our ability to communicate effectively and assertively in relationships. When we have a strong sense of self-worth and self-acceptance, we can express our thoughts, feelings, and needs openly and honestly. This promotes healthy communication, active listening, and emotional well-being, laying the foundation for understanding and connection with others.

Empathy and Compassion

Practicing self-love cultivates empathy and

compassion, which are essential qualities for meaningful relationships. When we love ourselves, we can extend that love and understanding to others. By empathizing with their experiences, validating their emotions, and showing compassion, we create a supportive and nurturing environment that fosters deep connections.

Growth and Support

Self-love encourages personal growth and self-improvement, which positively impacts our relationships. When we prioritize our growth, we become better equipped to support and uplift others in their own journeys. By continuously developing ourselves and supporting the growth of others, we foster an environment of mutual empowerment and encouragement.

Balance and Independence

Self-love allows us to maintain a healthy balance between our individuality and our connections with others. When we love ourselves, we understand the importance of self-care, personal boundaries, and maintaining our interests and passions. This balance promotes independence and autonomy within relationships, allowing each person to thrive and contribute authentically.

Self-love and meaningful relationships are deeply interconnected, each supporting and enhancing the other. By cultivating self-love, embracing authenticity, setting healthy boundaries, communicating effectively, practicing empathy and compassion, nurturing personal growth, and maintaining a healthy balance, we create the conditions for fulfilling and harmonious connections with others. Through the interplay of self-love and relationships, we embark on a journey of personal growth, mutual support, and deep fulfilment, creating a foundation for love and connection that nourishes both ourselves and those around us.

PART FIVE

PURSUING PASSION AND PURPOSE

"Whatever you do, work at it with all your heart, as working for the Lord, not for human masters." - Colossians 3:23

UNDERSTANDING PASSION AND PURPOSE

Passion and purpose are two interconnected concepts that drive our actions and bring meaning to our lives.

Passion refers to a strong and intense enthusiasm or interest in something. It is a deep-seated emotion that ignites our motivation, drives our creativity, and fuels our dedication towards a particular activity, goal, or pursuit. Passion is often associated with a sense of joy, fulfilment, and excitement. It can manifest in various areas of life, such as hobbies, career choices, relationships, or causes we deeply care about.

Purpose, on the other hand, involves finding a meaningful reason or calling behind our actions. It goes beyond personal fulfilment and encompasses a sense of contributing to something larger than ourselves. Purpose is about understanding our unique role and impact in the world and living in alignment with our values, strengths, and aspirations. It gives us a sense of direction, guiding our decisions and actions towards making a positive difference in our lives and the lives of others.

Passion and purpose are closely intertwined.

Passion often serves as the driving force behind discovering and pursuing our purpose. It fuels our commitment, perseverance, and enthusiasm as we engage in activities that align with our values and bring us joy. Purpose, in turn, gives depth and significance to our passions, helping us understand how our individual interests and talents can contribute to a greater purpose or make a positive impact in the world.

When we cultivate both passion and purpose in our lives, we experience a profound sense of fulfilment, meaning, and alignment. We feel inspired and motivated to pursue our goals, navigate challenges, and embrace opportunities for growth. Passion and purpose bring a sense of clarity, focus, and direction, guiding us towards a life that is deeply satisfying, purposeful, and in harmony with our authentic selves.

Ultimately, passion and purpose are deeply personal and can vary from person to person. It is a journey of self-discovery, reflection, and exploration to uncover what truly ignites our passion and aligns with our sense of purpose. By pursuing our passions and living in alignment with our purpose, we can create a life that is rich in meaning, fulfilment, and impact.

The pursuit of passion and purpose is a transformative journey that aligns our actions with our deepest desires and values. It calls us to engage in work, endeavours, and relationships with wholeheartedness and dedication. The quote from Colossians 3:23 reminds us to approach our endeavours with a sense of purpose, viewing them as opportunities to contribute meaningfully and make a difference. In this section, we will explore the significance of pursuing passion and purpose, the benefits it brings to our lives, and strategies for discovering and living in alignment with our true calling.

Discovering Personal Passions

Discovering our passions requires self-exploration and introspection. It involves reflecting on our

Passion often serves as the driving force behind discovering and pursuing our purpose.

interests, values, and curiosities. By identifying the activities and pursuits that bring us joy, fulfilment, and a sense of purpose, we can uncover our unique passions and chart a course towards a more meaningful life.

Aligning Work with Passion and Purpose

One of the significant aspects of pursuing passion and purpose is aligning our work with what truly inspires and motivates us. When we find work that resonates with our passions and allows us to express our purpose, it becomes more than just a job; it becomes a source of fulfilment and impact. We will explore strategies for exploring career paths that align with our passions and ways to infuse purpose into our current work.

Overcoming Obstacles and Fears

The pursuit of passion and purpose is not always a smooth path. It may involve facing challenges, doubts, and fears. However, by recognizing and addressing these obstacles, we can navigate through them and continue our journey towards a purposeful life. We will discuss strategies for overcoming self-doubt, fear of failure, and societal pressures that may hinder us from pursuing our passions and living in alignment with our purpose.

Cultivating Resilience and Persistence

The pursuit of passion and purpose requires resilience and persistence. It involves embracing setbacks and failures as opportunities for growth and learning. By developing resilience, we can bounce back from challenges, stay committed to our goals, and persist in the face of adversity.

Living a Purpose-Driven Life

Living in alignment with our passion and purpose brings a profound sense of fulfilment and joy. It involves making choices and taking actions that align with our values and contribute to something greater than ourselves. We will explore strategies for infusing purpose into all aspects of life, from relationships and personal growth to community involvement and service.

Embracing the Journey

The journey of pursuing passion and purpose is ongoing and evolving. It requires continuous self-reflection, adaptation, and growth. By embracing the process and allowing ourselves to evolve, we can create a life that is rich in meaning, purpose, and fulfilment.

Pursuing passion and purpose is a transformative endeavour that calls us to live with intention, wholeheartedness, and dedication. By aligning our actions with our deepest desires, values, and calling, we can create a life that is meaningful, purposeful, and deeply satisfying. Through self-exploration, overcoming obstacles, cultivating resilience, and embracing the journey, we can uncover our passions, live in alignment with our purpose, and make a positive impact in the world around us. The pursuit of passion and purpose is not only a personal journey but also a spiritual one, as we strive to work with all our heart, guided by our connection to something greater than ourselves.

DISCOVERING YOUR PASSIONS

Exploring techniques for identifying and uncovering your true passions and interests.

Self-Reflection: Take time for introspection and self-reflection to explore your likes, dislikes, and areas of curiosity. Ask yourself what activities bring you joy, energize you, and make you lose track of time. Reflect on moments in your life when you felt most fulfilled and alive. These reflections can help reveal patterns and themes that indicate your passions.

Try New Things: Step outside of your comfort zone and try new activities and experiences. Engage in a variety of hobbies, take classes, attend workshops, or join groups related to different interests. This exploration allows you to expose yourself to different experiences and discover new passions that resonate with you.

Pay Attention to Your Emotions: Notice how different activities and experiences make you feel. Pay attention to the emotions and sensations they evoke within you. Activities that spark enthusiasm, excitement, or a sense of flow are often indicators of your passions. Conversely, activities that consistently drain your energy or bring about negative emotions may not align with your true passions.

Reflect on Childhood Interests: Think back to your childhood and reflect on the activities or hobbies that captivated your attention. Childhood interests often provide clues about our inherent passions and natural inclinations. Revisit those interests and see if they still ignite a sense of joy and curiosity.

Seek Inspiration: Surround yourself with sources of inspiration, such as books, podcasts, documentaries, or conversations with passionate individuals. Exposing yourself to stories of people pursuing their passions can spark inspiration and provide insights into your own interests and aspirations.

Take Note of Peak Experiences: Reflect on moments in your life when you experienced a sense of accomplishment, fulfilment, or deep connection. What were you doing? What made those experiences so meaningful? These peak moments can indicate areas of passion and interest worth exploring further.

Embrace Curiosity: Cultivate a curious mindset and explore different topics, subjects, and areas of knowledge. Follow your curiosity and delve deeper into subjects that intrigue you. The pursuit of knowledge and exploration can often lead to the discovery of new passions.

Seek Feedback and Input: Ask trusted friends, family members, or mentors for their observations and insights regarding your strengths and interests. They may offer valuable perspectives and help you recognize passions you may not have considered.

Remember, discovering your passions is a process that takes time and exploration. Be patient with yourself and embrace the journey of self-discovery. Your passions may evolve and change over time, so stay open to new experiences and allow yourself the freedom to explore different paths. The key is to listen to your heart and follow what truly brings you joy, fulfilment, and a sense of purpose.

ALIGNING VALUES AND PASSIONS

Understanding the importance of aligning your values with your passions to create a sense of purpose and fulfilment.

Identify Your Core Values: Begin by clarifying your core values, which are the guiding principles that shape your beliefs, attitudes, and actions. Consider what principles and ideals are most important to you in life, such as honesty, compassion, creativity, or social justice. Reflect on the values that resonate deeply with you and align with your authentic self.

Assess Your Passions: Reflect on your passions

and interests that you identified during the process of discovering your passions. Examine how these passions align with your core values. Do they reflect and support the principles you hold dear? Consider whether engaging in these activities allows you to express and embody your values.

Seek Alignment: Explore how you can align your passions with your values. Look for opportunities to engage in activities that align with your core values and bring you joy and fulfilment. For example, if you value environmental sustainability, you might explore passions related to sustainable living, conservation, or advocacy for environmental causes.

Evaluate Your Current Pursuits: Assess the activities and commitments in your life to determine if they align with your values and passions. Identify any areas where there may be a misalignment and consider how you can make adjustments. This might involve letting go of activities or commitments that no longer resonate with your values or finding ways to infuse your current pursuits with aspects that align more closely with your passions and values.

Create a Personal Mission Statement: Craft a personal mission statement that encompasses your passions and values. This statement can serve as a guiding framework for your actions and decisions. It helps you stay focused on what matters most to you and ensures that your pursuits are in alignment with your core values and passions.

Reflect on the Impact: Consider the impact of aligning your values and passions. Recognize that when your actions align with your values, you experience a greater sense of purpose, fulfilment, and authenticity. Your pursuits become more meaningful because they reflect who you truly are and what you deeply care about. By aligning your passions with your values, you create a harmonious integration of your personal and authentic self.

Embrace Growth and Flexibility: Recognize that alignment between your values and passions is a continuous journey of growth and self-discovery. As you evolve and your values may shift, it is important to reassess and realign your passions accordingly. Stay open to new experiences, perspectives, and possibilities that may reshape your understanding of your values and passions.

Remember, the alignment of your values and passions is a deeply personal and individual process. It requires self-reflection, introspection, and ongoing exploration. When you align your values with your passions, you cultivate a strong sense of purpose and fulfilment, allowing you to lead a life that is authentic, meaningful, and in line with what truly matters to you.

OVERCOMING FEAR AND RESISTANCE

Strategies for overcoming fear, self-doubt, and societal pressures that may hinder the pursuit of your passions and purpose.

Recognize and Acknowledge Your Fears: Begin by identifying the specific fears, self-doubts, and limiting beliefs that are holding you back. Reflect on the thoughts and emotions that arise when you contemplate pursuing your passions or stepping into your purpose. By acknowledging and naming these fears, you can start to address them more effectively.

Challenge Negative Self-Talk: Pay attention to your inner dialogue and notice when self-doubt or negative self-talk arises. Replace self-critical thoughts with affirming and empowering statements. Remind yourself of your strengths, capabilities, and the value you bring. Practice self-compassion and kindness towards yourself, treating yourself with the same encouragement and support you would offer a loved one.

Embrace Failure as Growth: Shift your perspective on failure and view it as a natural part of the learning process. Understand that setbacks and mistakes are opportunities for growth and improvement. Embrace a mindset of resilience and learn from your experiences, allowing them to propel you forward rather than hold you back.

Surround Yourself with Supportive People: Seek out a supportive network of family, friends, mentors, or like-minded individuals who believe in you and your pursuits. Surrounding yourself with positive influences can help counteract external pressures and provide encouragement, guidance, and inspiration along your journey.

Take Small Steps and Celebrate Progress: Break down your goals into manageable steps and take consistent action. Start with small, achievable tasks that move you closer to your passions and purpose. Celebrate your progress along the way, no matter how small. Each step forward builds momentum and confidence, gradually reducing fear and resistance.

Visualize Success and Positivity: Create a clear mental image of yourself successfully pursuing your passions and living out your purpose. Visualize yourself overcoming challenges, embracing your strengths, and achieving your goals. Use visualization techniques to reinforce positive beliefs and cultivate a mindset of possibility and success.

Set Realistic Expectations: Recognize that pursuing your passions and purpose is a journey, and it may take time to achieve the outcomes you desire. Set realistic expectations and focus on the process rather than solely on the end result. Celebrate the small victories and progress you make along the way, appreciating the growth and learning that comes with each step.

Practice Self-Care and Mindfulness: Take care of your physical, mental, and emotional well-being. Engage in self-care practices that nourish and recharge you, such as exercise, meditation, journaling, or spending time in nature. Cultivate mindfulness to stay present and cantered, allowing you to navigate fear and resistance with greater clarity and resilience.

Challenge Societal Pressures: Recognize that societal pressures and expectations may influence your fears and resistance. Challenge societal norms and expectations that do not align with your authentic self and values. Remember that your passions and purpose are unique to you, and they may not conform to conventional ideas of success or fulfilment. Trust your own path and definition of what brings you joy and purpose.

Seek Professional Support: If fear, self-doubt, or resistance persist and significantly hinder your pursuit of passions and purpose, consider seeking professional support. A therapist, coach, or mentor can provide guidance, tools, and strategies to help you overcome obstacles, build confidence, and navigate challenges effectively.

By implementing these strategies, you can gradually overcome fear, self-doubt, and societal pressures that may hinder the pursuit of your passions and purpose. Remember that your passions and purpose are worth pursuing, and you have the inner strength and resilience to overcome any obstacles that come your way.

FINDING PURPOSE IN YOUR CAREER

Exploring ways to infuse purpose and meaning into your professional life, whether it's through finding a fulfilling job or creating your own path.

Reflect on Your Values and Passions: Start by reflecting on your core values and passions. Consider what brings you joy, fulfilment, and a sense of purpose. Think about the activities, causes, or issues that resonate with you on a deep level. Understanding your values and passions will guide you in aligning them with your career choices.

Identify Your Strengths and Talents: Take time to assess your unique strengths, talents, and skills. Identify what you excel at and enjoy doing.

Reflect on your past experiences, achievements, and feedback from others to gain insights into your strengths. Leveraging your strengths in your career can bring a sense of purpose and fulfilment.

Research and Explore: Conduct research to explore different industries, job roles, and career paths that align with your values, passions, and strengths. Learn about organizations and companies that prioritize social impact, sustainability, or other causes that resonate with you. Look for opportunities to combine your interests and skills with meaningful work.

Network and Seek Mentors: Build connections with professionals in fields or industries that align with your interests. Attend networking events, join professional organizations, and seek out mentors who can provide guidance and insights. Engaging with individuals who share similar values and are passionate about their work can help you gain valuable insights and opportunities.

Volunteer and Take on Side Projects: Consider volunteering or engaging in side projects that allow you to contribute to causes or issues that matter to you. This can provide valuable experience, expand your network, and help you develop skills relevant to your desired career path. Look for opportunities to apply your skills and make a positive impact outside of your current job.

Create Your Own Path: If you don't find existing job opportunities that align with your purpose, consider creating your own path. Entrepreneurship or freelancing may offer the flexibility and freedom to pursue your passions and create meaningful work. Start by identifying a problem or need in the world that you are passionate about addressing, and develop a business or project around it.

Seek Meaningful Work Environments: When searching for a job or considering a career change, look for organizations that prioritize purpose, employee well-being, and social impact. Research companies' mission statements, values, and company culture to determine if they align with your own values and aspirations. Seek out work environments that foster personal and professional growth and allow you to make a difference.

Continual Growth and Learning: Commit to lifelong learning and professional development.

Attend workshops, seminars, or online courses that can enhance your skills and knowledge in areas related to your purpose and career goals. Stay curious and open-minded, embracing new opportunities for growth and expanding your understanding of the world.

Reflect and Evaluate: Regularly assess your career journey and reflect on whether you are still aligned with your purpose and values. Take time to evaluate your progress, achievements, and areas of growth. Adjust your path if needed, making conscious choices that bring you closer to a career that embodies your purpose and brings you fulfilment.

Remember that finding purpose in your career is a dynamic and ongoing process. It may require exploration, experimentation, and adaptation along the way. Embrace the journey and trust that by infusing purpose and meaning into your professional life, you can experience a deep sense of fulfilment and contribute to making a positive impact in the world.

PURSUING PASSION OUTSIDE OF WORK

Recognizing the value of pursuing passions and hobbies outside of your career and incorporating them into your daily life for a well-rounded sense of purpose.

Rediscover Your Interests and Passions: Take time to reconnect with your interests and passions outside of work. Reflect on activities, hobbies, or causes that bring you joy and fulfilment. Consider what activities make you lose track of time or ignite a sense of excitement and enthusiasm.

Prioritize Self-Care and Personal Well-Being: Understand that pursuing passions outside of work is not only about productivity but also about personal well-being. Make self-care a priority, as it allows you to recharge, reduce stress, and maintain a healthy work-life balance. Engage in activities that promote relaxation, such as exercise, meditation, spending time in nature, or engaging in creative pursuits.

Make Time for Your Passions: Intentionally carve out time in your schedule for pursuing your passions. Treat your passions as important commitments and dedicate regular time to engage in activities that bring you joy. It could be a few hours each week or designated blocks of time during the weekends. Protect this time and make it a non-negotiable part of your routine.

Set Goals and Create a Plan: Define clear goals related to your passions and hobbies. What do you hope to achieve or experience? Break down these goals into smaller, actionable steps. Creating a plan will help you stay focused, motivated, and accountable in pursuing your passions.

Create a Supportive Environment: Surround yourself with like-minded individuals who share your interests and passions. Join clubs, organizations, or online communities related to your hobbies. Engaging with others who have similar interests can provide a sense of camaraderie, encouragement, and inspiration. It can also open doors to new opportunities and collaborations.

Embrace Continuous Learning: Deepen your knowledge and skills in your chosen passion or hobby through continuous learning. Take classes, workshops, or online courses to enhance your abilities and expand your understanding. Embrace the journey of lifelong learning, as it adds depth and richness to your pursuits.

Seek Balance and Variety: Explore a diverse range of passions and hobbies to find a well-rounded sense of purpose. Engaging in different activities can bring variety and prevent burnout. Allow yourself to explore new interests and be open to trying new things. Embrace the idea that passions can evolve and change over time, and be willing to adapt and explore different avenues.

Share Your Passions with Others: Find opportunities to share your passions with others. It could be through teaching, mentoring, volunteering, or creating content online. Sharing your knowledge and experiences not only contributes to the community but also deepens your own understanding and connection to your passions.

Embrace the Joy of the Process: Remember that pursuing passions outside of work is not solely about achieving specific outcomes. Embrace the joy of the process itself. Find fulfilment in the act of creation, exploration, and personal growth that comes from engaging with your passions. Allow yourself to savour each moment and appreciate the journey.

Practice Mindfulness and Gratitude: Cultivate mindfulness in your pursuits by staying present and fully engaged in the activities you enjoy. Practice gratitude for the opportunity to pursue your passions and experience joy outside of work. Reflect on the positive impact these activities have on your overall well-being and sense of purpose.

By incorporating your passions and hobbies into your daily life, you can experience a well-rounded sense of purpose, fulfilment, and personal growth. Pursuing passions outside of work allows you to tap into different aspects of your identity and nourish your soul, ultimately enhancing your overall well-being and quality of life.

BALANCING MULTIPLE PASSIONS
Strategies for managing and harmonizing multiple passions and interests to find fulfilment and avoid overwhelm.

Prioritize and Identify Core Passions: Reflect on

your multiple passions and identify the ones that are most important to you. Prioritize these passions based on your values, level of engagement, and long-term fulfilment. This will help you focus your time and energy on the passions that truly matter to you.

Create a Schedule and Set Boundaries: Establish a schedule that allows you to dedicate time to each of your passions. Set clear boundaries to ensure that you have designated periods for each interest without overextending yourself. This will help you maintain balance and prevent overwhelm.

Embrace Flexibility and Adaptability: Recognize that your passions may evolve over time. Be open to adapting your schedule and priorities as needed. Allow yourself the freedom to explore new interests or shift focus when necessary. Embracing flexibility will help you adapt to changing circumstances and discover new passions along the way.

Look for Synergies and Cross-Pollination: Seek opportunities to integrate your different passions and find common ground between them. Look for connections, themes, or skills that overlap across your interests. This can create a sense of coherence and synergy, making it easier to manage and harmonize multiple passions.

Delegate and Collaborate: If you find that managing multiple passions becomes overwhelming, consider delegating certain tasks or collaborating with others who share similar interests. This can help distribute the workload and allow you to focus on the aspects of your passions that bring you the most joy and fulfilment.

Practice Time Management and Prioritization: Develop effective time management skills to maximize productivity and allocate time for each passion. Prioritize tasks and activities based on their importance and urgency. Set realistic goals and break them down into manageable steps to stay organized and focused.

Practice Self-Care and Mindfulness: Take care of yourself physically, mentally, and emotionally. Prioritize self-care activities that rejuvenate and recharge you. Incorporate mindfulness practices into your daily routine to stay present, reduce stress, and enhance your overall well-being. This will help you maintain a healthy balance while pursuing multiple passions.

Seek Support and Accountability: Surround yourself with a supportive network of friends, family, or like-minded individuals who can offer encouragement, guidance, and accountability. Share your goals and aspirations with them, and seek their support in managing your multiple passions. Having a support system can provide valuable insights and help keep you motivated and focused.

Embrace the Process and Enjoy the Journey: Remember that managing multiple passions is a journey, not a destination. Embrace the process, enjoy the exploration, and celebrate small victories along the way. Find joy in the learning, growth, and self-expression that come from pursuing your passions. Appreciate the diversity and richness that multiple passions bring to your life.

Regularly Assess and Reflect: Periodically assess and reflect on your commitments and passions. Evaluate if certain interests are still bringing you fulfilment and aligning with your values. Adjust your priorities and commitments accordingly, letting go of passions that no longer serve you and making room for new ones that ignite your enthusiasm.

Finding balance and fulfilment while managing multiple passions is a continuous process of self-discovery and self-awareness. By implementing these strategies and remaining adaptable, you can create a harmonious and fulfilling life that embraces your diverse interests and passion.

TURNING PASSION INTO ACTION

Practical steps and approaches to transform your passions into tangible goals and actions that lead to meaningful outcomes.

Clarify Your Vision: Start by clearly defining your passion and identifying the specific outcomes or goals you want to achieve. Visualize what success looks like for you and articulate it in a clear and concise manner. This clarity will provide a solid foundation for taking action.

Set SMART Goals: Break down your passion-driven vision into specific, measurable, achievable, relevant, and time-bound (SMART) goals. SMART goals provide a framework for creating actionable steps that move you closer to your desired outcomes. Ensure that your goals align with your passion and are realistic and attainable.

Create an Action Plan: Develop a detailed action plan that outlines the specific steps you need to take to achieve your goals. Break down each goal into smaller tasks or milestones and establish a timeline for completing them. This plan serves as a roadmap to guide your actions and keep you on track.

Take Consistent Action: Consistency is key to turning passion into action. Commit to taking regular and consistent steps towards your goals. Even small actions can accumulate over time and contribute to significant progress. Set aside dedicated time each day or week to work on your passion and hold yourself accountable to follow through.

Seek Knowledge and Skill Development: Identify the knowledge and skills needed to excel in your passion area. Take proactive steps to acquire the necessary expertise through self-study, research, formal education, mentorship, or workshops.

Continuously seek opportunities for personal and professional growth to enhance your capabilities and effectiveness.

Break Through Barriers: Recognize and address any barriers or obstacles that may hinder your progress. These could be internal, such as self-doubt or fear of failure, or external, such as limited resources or time constraints. Develop strategies to overcome these challenges, such as seeking support, developing resilience, or finding alternative solutions.

Cultivate a Growth Mindset: Adopt a growth mindset, which embraces challenges, sees setbacks as opportunities for learning, and believes in the potential for personal growth and development. Embrace a positive and optimistic attitude, and view failures or setbacks as valuable lessons that can propel you forward on your passion-driven journey.

Network and Collaborate: Surround yourself with like-minded individuals who share your passion or are working in related fields. Network with professionals, join relevant communities or organizations, and attend events or conferences to expand your connections. Collaborate with others who can offer support, guidance, or opportunities for collaboration, and leverage collective knowledge and resources.

Evaluate and Adjust: Regularly assess your progress and evaluate the effectiveness of your actions. Reflect on what is working well and what needs adjustment. Be open to adapting your approach and making necessary changes to ensure continued growth and alignment with your passion-driven goals.

Celebrate Milestones and Successes: Acknowledge and celebrate your achievements along the way. Recognize and reward yourself for reaching milestones or making significant progress. Celebrating your successes reinforces your motivation, boosts confidence, and provides a sense of fulfilment, further fuelling your passion-driven actions.

Remember that turning passion into action is a dynamic and ongoing process. Stay connected to your passion, remain adaptable, and be willing to adjust your goals and actions as you gain new insights and experiences. By taking practical steps and consistently moving forward, you can transform your passion into meaningful outcomes and create a life that is deeply aligned with your authentic self.

Overcoming Obstacles:

Navigating challenges and setbacks on the journey of pursuing passion and purpose, and developing resilience and perseverance.

Embrace a Growth Mindset: Adopt a mindset that views challenges as opportunities for growth and learning. Instead of being discouraged by setbacks, see them as stepping stones towards success. Cultivate a belief in your ability to overcome obstacles and develop resilience in the face of adversity.

Reframe Failure: Shift your perspective on failure. Rather than seeing it as a reflection of your worth or a definitive outcome, view it as a valuable learning experience. Understand that setbacks and failures are normal parts of any journey and use them as opportunities to learn, adapt, and improve.

Set Realistic Expectations: Recognize that pursuing passion and purpose is a process that takes time, effort, and perseverance. Set realistic expectations for yourself and understand that progress may not always be linear. Be patient and allow yourself the space to learn and grow along the way.

Seek Support: Reach out for support from others who can offer guidance, encouragement, and perspective. Surround yourself with a network of mentors, friends, or like-minded individuals who can provide advice, accountability, and emotional support. Lean on their wisdom and experiences to navigate challenges and stay motivated.

Break Challenges into Manageable Steps: When faced with a daunting obstacle, break it down into smaller, more manageable steps. This approach makes the challenge appear less overwhelming and allows you to focus on one step at a time. Celebrate each small victory as you progress towards overcoming the larger obstacle.

Practice Self-Compassion: Be kind and compassionate towards yourself during difficult times. Acknowledge that setbacks and obstacles are a natural part of the journey. Treat yourself with understanding, patience, and self-care. Use self-compassion as a source of strength and motivation to keep moving forward.

Learn from Setbacks: Take the time to reflect on setbacks and setbacks, and identify the lessons they offer. Analyze what went wrong, what could be done differently, and what you can learn from the experience. Use these insights to adjust your approach and make informed decisions as you continue pursuing your passion and purpose.

Cultivate Resilience: Build your resilience by developing coping mechanisms and strategies to bounce back from setbacks. Practice stress management techniques, engage in activities that rejuvenate you, and maintain a positive mindset. Cultivating resilience will help you weather challenges and stay focused on your goals.

Stay Flexible and Adapt: Recognize that the path to pursuing passion and purpose may not always be linear or predictable. Be open to adjusting your plans and adapting to changing circumstances. Embrace flexibility, embrace new opportunities, and be willing to make course corrections as needed.

Keep the Big Picture in Mind: When facing challenges, remind yourself of the bigger picture and the reasons why you are pursuing your passion and purpose. Reconnect with your sense of purpose and the impact you want to make. This can provide the motivation and determination needed to overcome obstacles and stay committed to your journey.

Remember that overcoming obstacles is an integral part of the pursuit of passion and purpose. It is through facing and overcoming challenges that we grow, learn, and become stronger. Embrace the journey, stay resilient, and maintain a positive mindset as you navigate obstacles on your path to living a purposeful life.

CULTIVATING A GROWTH MINDSET

Embracing a growth mindset to foster continuous learning, personal growth, and the exploration of new passions and purposes.

Understand the Power of Beliefs: Recognize that

your beliefs about intelligence, abilities, and talents can shape your mindset. Embrace the idea that intelligence and abilities can be developed through effort, learning, and practice. Believe in your potential for growth and improvement.

Embrace Challenges: Embrace challenges as opportunities for growth rather than seeing them as threats or obstacles. Embrace the mindset that challenges provide valuable learning experiences and opportunities to expand your skills and knowledge. Embrace a "can-do" attitude and view challenges as exciting chances to stretch yourself.

Emphasize Effort and Persistence: Focus on the process and effort you put into learning and improving rather than solely on the outcome. Recognize that effort and perseverance are key factors in achieving success and developing new skills. Embrace the mindset that with continued effort and dedication, you can overcome obstacles and achieve your goals.

Embrace Failure as Learning: Embrace failure as an essential part of the learning process. Instead of seeing failure as a reflection of your abilities, view it as an opportunity to learn, grow, and make adjustments. Embrace a mindset that sees failure as a stepping stone towards success, and use it as a chance to gather feedback and improve.

Cultivate Curiosity and Love for Learning: Foster a sense of curiosity and a love for learning new things. Embrace the mindset that there is always more to discover and explore. Approach new experiences with an open mind and a willingness to learn from them. Seek out opportunities for growth and actively pursue new knowledge and skills.

Embrace Feedback: Welcome feedback as a valuable source of information and insight. See feedback as an opportunity for growth and improvement rather than criticism. Embrace a mindset that values constructive feedback and uses it to make adjustments and refine your skills and approaches.

Surround Yourself with Growth-Oriented Individuals: Surround yourself with individuals who also have a growth mindset. Engage in conversations and interactions with people who inspire and encourage you to embrace growth and learning. Learn from their experiences and share your own, fostering an environment of continuous growth and support.

Focus on Personal Development: Prioritize personal development and continuous learning. Set goals for yourself that align with your passions and interests, and commit to consistently learning and growing in those areas. Embrace a mindset that sees personal growth as a lifelong journey rather than a destination.

Practice Resilience: Build resilience by viewing setbacks as temporary and surmountable obstacles. Embrace challenges as opportunities to learn, adapt, and grow. Develop strategies to bounce back from setbacks and setbacks, and cultivate a positive and optimistic attitude in the face of adversity.

Celebrate Progress and Achievements: Celebrate your progress and achievements along the way. Embrace a mindset that values the journey and recognizes the milestones and accomplishments, no matter how small. Take the time to acknowledge your growth and use it as motivation to continue pursuing new passions and purposes.

By cultivating a growth mindset, you open yourself

up to new possibilities, embrace continuous learning, and foster personal growth. With a growth mindset, you can explore new passions and purposes, adapt to challenges, and continually develop your skills and abilities. Embrace the mindset that your potential is not fixed, and that through effort and dedication, you can continually expand your horizons and live a fulfilling and purposeful life.

IMPACTING OTHERS

Exploring ways to use your passions and purpose to make a positive impact on others, whether through mentorship, volunteering, or activism.

Identify Your Areas of Passion: Reflect on the causes or social issues that ignite a fire within you. Consider your unique talents, skills, and interests that can be aligned with making a positive impact. Identify the areas where you feel most passionate and where you believe you can contribute effectively.

Seek Volunteer Opportunities: Look for volunteer opportunities that align with your passions and purpose. Whether it's working with a local non-profit, joining community initiatives, or contributing your skills pro bono, volunteering can provide meaningful opportunities to make a difference. Research organizations or causes that resonate with you and reach out to explore how you can contribute.

Mentorship and Guidance: Share your knowledge and experiences with others by becoming a mentor or offering guidance to individuals who can benefit from your expertise. Mentorship provides an opportunity to support and empower others on their own journeys, whether it's in their career, personal growth, or pursuing their passions.

Use Your Voice: Speak up and advocate for causes that align with your values. Use your platform, whether it's through social media, public speaking engagements, or joining advocacy groups, to raise awareness and influence positive change. Engage in conversations and initiatives that promote inclusivity, equality, sustainability, and social justice.

Create Meaningful Projects: Initiate your own

projects or initiatives that address social issues or contribute to the well-being of others. Use your creativity and skills to develop innovative solutions or programs that make a positive impact. Collaborate with like-minded individuals or organizations to amplify your efforts and expand your reach.

Support Socially Responsible Businesses: Align your consumer choices with your values by supporting businesses and organizations that prioritize social responsibility. Choose companies that have sustainable practices, give back to communities, or support causes that resonate with you. By making intentional choices, you can contribute to creating a positive impact through your everyday actions.

Engage in Active Listening: Take the time to truly listen and understand the needs and perspectives of others. Show empathy and compassion as you interact with individuals and communities. By actively listening, you can better understand how to support and address the specific needs of others, and tailor your efforts to create a more meaningful impact.

Collaborate and Network: Build connections with like-minded individuals and organizations who share similar passions and goals. Collaborate on projects or initiatives that can create a collective impact. By working together, you can combine your strengths, resources, and expertise to make a more significant difference in the lives of others.

Continuously Learn and Grow: Stay informed about the issues you care about and seek opportunities for personal growth and education. Attend workshops, seminars, or courses related to social impact and advocacy. Continuously expand your knowledge and skills to become more effective in making a positive impact.

Lead by Example: Live your passions and purpose authentically. Be a role model by embodying the values and principles you believe in. Inspire others through your actions and choices. Your genuine commitment to making a positive impact can motivate and encourage others to do the same.

Remember, the impact you make doesn't have to be grandiose or on a large scale. Small acts of kindness, daily gestures of support, and consistent efforts to contribute positively can create ripple effects and inspire others to take action. By using your passions and purpose to make a difference, you can leave a meaningful impact on the lives of others and contribute to a more compassionate and thriving world.

PART SIX

OVERCOMING LONELINESS AND EMBRACING SOLITUDE

"Be still before the Lord and wait patiently for him."

- Psalm 37:7

In our fast-paced and interconnected world, it is not uncommon to experience moments of loneliness and a longing for deeper connection. However, amidst the hustle and bustle of daily life, there is a space for solitude—an opportunity to embrace and find solace in being alone. Solitude is not synonymous with loneliness; instead, it is a conscious choice to find inner peace, reflection, and renewal. It is a time for self-discovery, self-care, and a deeper connection with oneself and the divine.

Loneliness, often characterized by a sense of isolation and longing for companionship, can affect individuals from all walks of life. It can stem from various factors, such as social disconnection, a lack of meaningful relationships, or a feeling of not being understood or valued. However, it is important to recognize that loneliness is not a permanent state but rather a temporary experience that can be overcome through intentional practices and embracing the power of solitude.

In contrast, solitude is a state of being alone that is intentionally chosen and embraced. It is a time to disconnect from external distractions and immerse oneself in introspection, self-reflection, and self-care. Solitude provides an opportunity to explore one's thoughts, emotions, and desires without the influence of others' opinions or expectations. It allows for a deep connection with one's inner self, fostering self-awareness, personal growth, and a greater understanding of one's values and purpose.

By understanding the distinction between loneliness and solitude, we can shift our perspective and transform moments of aloneness into meaningful and enriching experiences. Overcoming loneliness involves recognizing the underlying causes, seeking connection and support from others, and devel oping healthy and fulfilling relationships. Embracing solitude, on the other hand, involves nurturing a sense of self-compassion, practicing self-

> By understanding the distinction between loneliness and solitude, we can shift our perspective and transform moments of aloneness into meaningful and enriching experiences.

care, and finding joy and fulfilment in spending quality time with oneself.

Throughout this exploration of overcoming loneliness and embracing solitude, we will delve into various subtopics that can empower individuals to navigate their journey towards self-discovery and inner peace. We will explore practical strategies for finding solace in solitude, nurturing meaningful connections, and discovering the beauty and strength that can be found within ourselves. Through this journey, we can uncover the transformative power of embracing solitude, fostering self-love, and creating a harmonious balance between solitude and meaningful connections with others.

As we embark on this exploration, we are reminded of the wisdom found in the scripture: "Be still before the Lord and wait patiently for him." In moments of solitude, we can find stillness, patience, and a deeper connection with the divine. By embracing solitude and overcoming loneliness, we can embark on a path of self-discovery, personal growth, and a profound sense of inner peace and fulfilment.

UNDERSTANDING LONELINESS

Exploring the nature of loneliness, its causes, and its impact on our mental, emotional, and physical well-being.

Loneliness is a complex and universal human emotion that can be characterized by a sense of isolation, disconnection, and longing for meaningful social interaction and companionship. It is important to understand that loneliness is not solely determined by the absence of people around us but rather by the perceived lack of deep and meaningful connections.

The causes of loneliness can vary and may include factors such as:

Social Isolation: When individuals lack regular social interactions, whether due to physical distance, a change in circumstances, or a lack of social networks, they may experience loneliness.

Transitions and Life Changes: Events such as moving to a new location, starting a new job, ending a relationship, or experiencing the loss of a loved one can disrupt existing social connections and contribute to feelings of loneliness.

Lack of Intimacy and Connection: Loneliness can stem from a lack of close relationships or the absence of meaningful emotional connections with others, leaving individuals feeling isolated and unfulfilled.

Alienation and Exclusion: Feeling excluded or marginalized due to factors such as discrimination, prejudice, or not fitting into societal norms can contribute to feelings of loneliness.

The impact of loneliness goes beyond just emotional discomfort. It can have significant effects on mental, emotional, and physical well-being, including:

Mental Health: Persistent loneliness is associated with an increased risk of developing mental health conditions such as depression, anxiety, and low self-esteem. It can also exacerbate existing mental health issues.

Emotional Well-being: Loneliness can lead to feelings of sadness, emptiness, and a lack of fulfilment. It can affect one's overall mood, self-worth, and ability to experience joy and contentment.

Physical Health: Research suggests that chronic loneliness can have adverse effects on physical health, including increased inflammation, weakened immune system functioning, and higher rates of cardiovascular problems.

Cognitive Function: Prolonged feelings of loneliness can impact cognitive function, including memory, attention, and decision-making abilities.

Understanding the nature and impact of loneliness is crucial for addressing and overcoming it. By recognizing the factors that contribute to loneliness and its effects on our well-being, we can take proactive steps to cultivate meaningful connections, seek support, and develop strategies to combat loneliness in our lives.

THE DIFFERENCE BETWEEN LONELINESS AND SOLITUDE

Examining the distinction between loneliness and solitude, and understanding how solitude can be a source of strength and renewal.

While loneliness and solitude both involve being alone, there is a distinct difference between the two experiences.

Loneliness refers to a state of feeling disconnected, isolated, and lacking meaningful social connections. It is often accompanied by a deep longing for companionship and a sense of being misunderstood or unseen. Loneliness is primarily characterized by negative emotions and a perceived absence of desired social interaction. It can be distressing and have a detrimental impact on mental and emotional well-being.

On the other hand, solitude is a deliberate and voluntary choice to spend time alone, enjoying one's company. Solitude is a state of being at peace with oneself, free from external distractions, and open to self-reflection, introspection, and personal growth. It is a conscious decision to seek solitude as a means of rejuvenation, self-discovery, and renewal.

While loneliness is often associated with negative emotions, solitude can be seen as a positive and enriching experience. It allows individuals to connect with their inner selves, explore their thoughts and emotions, and engage in activities that bring them joy and fulfilment. Solitude can provide a sense of calm, clarity, and self-awareness.

One key distinction between loneliness and solitude lies in the sense of control and fulfilment. Loneliness is often perceived

as something beyond one's control, a state of lacking companionship despite a desire for it. In contrast, solitude is a deliberate choice and can be embraced as a valuable opportunity for self-care and personal growth.

Moreover, solitude can serve as a foundation for healthy social connections. By spending time alone and nurturing a positive relationship with oneself, individuals can better understand their own needs, values, and boundaries. This self-awareness can enhance the quality of their relationships with others and contribute to more meaningful connections.

It's important to note that the experience of

solitude can vary among individuals. Some may find solace in solitary activities such as reading, writing, or engaging in hobbies, while others may seek solitude in natural environments or through meditation and mindfulness practices.

By recognizing the difference between loneliness and solitude, individuals can embrace the potential benefits of solitude, integrating it into their lives as a source of strength, self-discovery, and personal well-being.

Exploring the Root Causes of Loneliness:
Identifying the underlying factors that contribute to feelings of loneliness, such as social disconnection, transitions, loss, or a lack of meaningful relationships.

Loneliness can stem from various root causes, and understanding these underlying factors is essential in addressing and overcoming feelings of isolation. Here are some common root causes of loneliness:

Social Disconnection: A lack of social connections or a small social network can contribute to feelings of loneliness. This may occur when individuals have limited opportunities for social interaction or when they struggle to form and maintain meaningful relationships.

Transitions and Life Changes: Major life transitions, such as moving to a new city, starting college, changing jobs, or experiencing the loss of a loved one, can disrupt social networks and leave individuals feeling disconnected and isolated.

Loss and Grief: The loss of a significant relationship through a breakup, divorce, or death can result in profound feelings of loneliness. Grief and the absence of a familiar presence can intensify the sense of isolation and longing for companionship.

Lack of Intimacy and Meaningful Connections: Loneliness can arise when individuals lack deep and meaningful relationships characterized by emotional intimacy, trust, and mutual understanding. Superficial or unfulfilling social interactions may not adequately meet one's need for connection, leading to a sense of loneliness.

Social Rejection and Isolation: Experiences of social rejection, exclusion, or discrimination can significantly contribute to loneliness. Feeling ostracized or disconnected due to factors such as race, ethnicity, sexual orientation, or other aspects of identity can lead to profound feelings of isolation.

Incompatible Social Environments: Some individuals may feel lonely due to a mismatch between their interests, values, or beliefs and the social environment they find themselves in. When one's authentic self is not fully embraced or when they struggle to find like-minded individuals, loneliness can result.

Technology and Social Media: Paradoxically, the rise of technology and social media can contribute to feelings of loneliness. While these platforms provide opportunities for connection, excessive reliance on virtual interactions and a lack of meaningful in-person connections can lead to a sense of isolation.

Mental Health Conditions: Certain mental health conditions, such as depression, social anxiety, or low self-esteem, can contribute to feelings of loneliness. These conditions may impact an individual's ability to initiate or maintain social connections, perpetuating a cycle of isolation.

It is important to recognize that loneliness can be influenced by a combination of these factors and may vary from person to person. By identifying the root causes of loneliness, individuals can gain insights into their own experiences and begin to take steps towards building meaningful connections, seeking support, and creating a social environment that fosters genuine connection and belonging.

DEVELOPING A HEALTHY RELATIONSHIP WITH SOLITUDE

Learning to embrace solitude as a conscious choice for self-reflection, self-care, and personal growth, and understanding the benefits it can bring to our lives.

Developing a healthy relationship with solitude involves recognizing and embracing its value as a conscious choice for self-reflection, self-care, and personal growth. Here are some key aspects to consider in cultivating a positive connection with solitude-

Self-Awareness: Start by gaining a deeper understanding of yourself and your needs. Reflect on what activities, environments, or moments bring you a sense of peace, clarity, and fulfilment when you are alone. This self-awareness will help you identify the types of solitude that resonate with you.

Intentional Time Alone: Set aside intentional periods of solitude in your schedule. Treat this time as a sacred practice dedicated to self-reflection, introspection, and rejuvenation. Create a space where you can engage in activities that bring you joy, such as reading, journaling, practicing mindfulness, or pursuing hobbies that nourish your soul.

Embracing Silence: Embrace moments of silence and stillness. Silence allows us to connect with our inner selves, listen to our thoughts and emotions, and gain clarity. Consider incorporating silent moments into your daily routine, such as practicing meditation, taking mindful walks, or simply finding a quiet space to be present with your thoughts.

Mindful Engagement: Engage in activities mindfully, even when you are alone. Whether it's cooking, exercising, or engaging in creative pursuits, be fully present in the moment, savouring the experience and cultivating a deeper connection with yourself. Mindful engagement enhances the richness of solitude and helps you fully embrace the present.

Self-Care and Nurturing: Use solitude as an opportunity for self-care and self-nurturing. Prioritize activities that replenish your energy, bring you joy, and align with your needs. This might include taking care of your physical health, engaging in hobbies, pampering yourself, or engaging in practices that promote emotional well-being, such as gratitude or self-compassion exercises.

Reflection and Growth: Solitude provides a space for self-reflection and personal growth. Use this time to explore your values, beliefs, and aspirations. Reflect on your goals, dreams, and areas of personal development. Set intentions for your growth and take small steps towards manifesting them.

Reconnecting with Nature: Spend time alone in nature, immersing yourself in its beauty and tranquillity. Nature offers a serene and grounding environment that can foster introspection and a sense of connection to something greater than ourselves.

Balancing Solitude and Social Connection:

While solitude is valuable, it's also important to strike a balance with social connections. Seek opportunities to engage in meaningful interactions with others, fostering relationships that nourish and support you. Connecting with others can complement and enhance the benefits of solitude.

By developing a healthy relationship with solitude, you can tap into its transformative power. Embracing solitude as a conscious choice allows for self-discovery, self-care, and personal growth, enabling you to nurture a deeper connection with yourself and find a sense of inner peace and fulfilment.

Nurturing Authentic Connections:

Exploring strategies for building and nurturing meaningful relationships that provide companionship, understanding, and support, thereby reducing feelings of loneliness.

Nurturing authentic connections is a vital aspect of overcoming loneliness and fostering a sense of companionship, understanding, and support. Here are some strategies for building and nurturing meaningful relationships-

Authenticity and Vulnerability: Be authentic

and vulnerable in your interactions with others. Share your true thoughts, feelings, and experiences. By opening up and being genuine, you create space for deeper connections and encourage others to do the same.

Active Listening: Practice active listening when engaging with others. Give your full attention, show genuine interest, and empathize with their experiences. Validate their feelings and perspectives, fostering a sense of understanding and connection.

Shared Interests and Activities: Engage in activities and join communities cantered around shared interests. Whether it's joining a club, participating in a hobby group, or attending events, connecting with others who share your passions can facilitate meaningful connections and provide a sense of belonging.

Quality Time: Prioritize quality time with the people you care about. Create opportunities for meaningful interactions, such as shared meals, walks, or engaging in activities together. Dedicate focused time to connect and deepen your relationships.

Open Communication: Foster open and honest

communication within your relationships. Encourage dialogue, express your needs and boundaries, and create a safe space for others to do the same. Clear communication helps build trust and understanding.

Mutual Support: Offer and seek support from your loved ones. Be there for others in their times of need, and don't hesitate to ask for help when you require it. Building a support network that provides mutual support and encouragement is essential for reducing feelings of loneliness.

Cultivate Empathy and Compassion: Practice empathy and compassion towards others. Seek to understand their experiences, perspectives, and emotions. Show kindness and compassion, and be willing to lend a helping hand when needed. These qualities foster deeper connections and create a supportive network.

Healthy Boundaries: Maintain healthy boundaries within your relationships. Clearly communicate your needs, and respect the boundaries of others. Establishing and respecting boundaries promotes mutual respect and fosters healthier, more balanced connections.

Regular Check-Ins: Regularly check in with your

loved ones to see how they're doing and let them know that you care. This simple act of reaching out and showing genuine interest can strengthen your relationships and help reduce feelings of isolation.

Quality over Quantity: Focus on the quality of your relationships rather than the quantity. Cultivate a few deep and meaningful connections rather than spreading yourself thin. Investing time and energy in nurturing a few authentic relationships can provide the support and companionship needed to combat loneliness.

Remember, building and nurturing meaningful relationships takes time and effort. Be patient, and allow connections to develop naturally. Embrace vulnerability, practice active listening, and foster a sense of empathy and compassion. By prioritizing authentic connections, you can reduce feelings of loneliness and cultivate a network of relationships that bring joy, understanding, and support into your life.

CULTIVATING SELF-COMPASSION AND SELF-ACCEPTANCE

Developing a compassionate and accepting relationship with ourselves, honouring our needs, and fostering a sense of self-love and worthiness.

Cultivating self-compassion and self-acceptance is an essential journey towards developing a compassionate and loving relationship with ourselves. Here are some strategies for cultivating self-compassion and self-acceptance-

Practice Self-Kindness: Treat yourself with kindness, just as you would treat a dear friend. Be gentle and understanding with yourself when facing challenges or setbacks. Replace self-criticism with self-encouragement and self-compassion.

Nurture Self-Care: Prioritize self-care and self-nurturing activities. Engage in practices that promote your physical, mental, and emotional well-being. This could include activities like getting enough rest, engaging in hobbies you enjoy, practicing mindfulness or meditation, and engaging in self-reflection.

Challenge Self-Judgment: Become aware of self-judgmental thoughts and beliefs and challenge them. Recognize that everyone makes mistakes and has flaws. Replace self-judgment with self-compassion, understanding that imperfections are a natural part of being human.

Practice Mindfulness: Cultivate a non-judgmental awareness of your thoughts, emotions, and sensations in the present moment. Mindfulness helps you observe your experiences without harsh judgment or avoidance. It allows you to acknowledge and accept whatever arises within you.

Embrace Imperfections: Embrace your imperfections and see them as part of your unique journey. Recognize that imperfections are opportunities for growth and learning. Embrace self-acceptance by acknowledging that you are worthy and deserving of love and acceptance, regardless of your perceived flaws.

Set Healthy Boundaries: Establish and maintain healthy boundaries in your relationships and daily life. Respect your needs and limitations, and communicate them assertively. Setting boundaries protects your well-being and fosters self-respect.

Celebrate Your Accomplishments: Acknowledge and celebrate your achievements, both big and small. Recognize your strengths and the progress you have made in your personal growth journey. Celebrating your accomplishments boosts self-confidence and reinforces self-acceptance.

Surround Yourself with Positive Influences: Surround yourself with people who uplift and support you. Seek out relationships and communities that promote positivity, acceptance, and personal growth. Surrounding yourself with positive influences can help reinforce self-compassion and self-acceptance.

Practice Gratitude: Cultivate a gratitude practice to shift your focus towards what you appreciate about yourself and your life. Regularly acknowledge and express gratitude for your strengths, qualities, and the experiences that have shaped you.

Seek Support: Reach out for support when needed. Whether it's from friends, family, or a therapist, seeking support can provide valuable insights and guidance as you navigate the journey of self-compassion and self-acceptance.

Remember, cultivating self-compassion and self-acceptance is a continuous practice that requires patience and self-reflection. Be kind to yourself throughout the process and embrace the inherent worthiness within you. By developing a compassionate and accepting relationship with yourself, you can foster a deep sense of self-love and worthiness that positively impacts all aspects of your life.

PRACTICES FOR FINDING SOLACE IN SOLITUDE

Discovering techniques and activities that can be enjoyed in moments of solitude, such as journaling, meditation, creative expression, and nature immersion.

Finding solace in solitude can be a powerful and enriching experience. Here are some practices that can help you embrace and enjoy your moments of solitude-

Journaling: Set aside time to engage in journaling, where you can freely express your thoughts, emotions, and reflections. Use this as an opportunity for self-discovery, self-reflection, and gaining clarity about your inner world.

Meditation: Explore different forms of meditation to cultivate inner peace and stillness. Whether it's focused breathing, mindfulness meditation, or guided visualizations, meditation can help quiet the mind, reduce stress, and deepen your connection with yourself.

Creative Expression: Engage in activities that allow you to express yourself creatively, such as painting, writing, playing an instrument, or crafting. Creativity provides an outlet for self-expression, emotional release, and self-discovery.

Nature Immersion: Spend time in nature and immerse yourself in its beauty. Take walks in the park, hike in the mountains, or sit by the beach. Nature has a way of grounding and calming our minds, helping us connect with something greater than ourselves.

Mindful Self-Care: Practice self-care activities that bring you joy and relaxation. This could include taking soothing baths, practicing yoga or stretching, reading a book, or listening to calming music. Prioritize activities that nurture your physical, mental, and emotional well-being.

Engage in Solitary Hobbies: Discover and engage in hobbies that you can enjoy on your own, such as gardening, photography, cooking, or playing an instrument. These activities allow you to focus your energy and attention, bringing a sense of fulfilment and accomplishment.

Mindful Walking: Take mindful walks where you focus your attention on the present moment and your surroundings. Pay attention to the sensations in your body, the sights, sounds, and smells around you. Walking mindfully can help you feel more grounded and connected with the world around you.

Reflection and Self-Exploration: Use your moments of solitude for introspection and self-exploration. Ask yourself meaningful questions about your values, goals, dreams, and aspirations. Take the time to understand yourself on a deeper level and gain insights into your life's direction.

Reading and Learning: Dive into books, articles, or podcasts that align with your interests and passions. Engaging in intellectual and personal growth can be both enriching and fulfilling. Use your solitude to expand your knowledge and explore new ideas.

Mindful Technology Use: Disconnect from technology for a while and create intentional periods of digital detox. Use this time to focus on yourself, your thoughts, and your experiences without the distractions of screens and social media.

Remember that the key to finding solace in solitude is to embrace it as a valuable and rejuvenating experience. Allow yourself the space and time to connect with your inner self, explore your interests, and recharge. Each individual's path to finding solace in solitude may be different, so find practices that resonate with you and bring you a sense of peace and fulfilment.

SEEKING SUPPORT AND CONNECTION

Recognizing the importance of seeking support from others, whether through therapy, support groups, or reaching out to trusted friends and family members.

Seeking support and connection is an essential part of navigating solitude and overcoming loneliness. Here are some ways you can reach out and cultivate meaningful connections with others-

Therapy or Counselling: Consider seeking the support of a therapist or counsellor. A professional can provide a safe space for you to explore your feelings, gain insights, and develop coping strategies. They can help you navigate through any challenges or emotional difficulties you may be facing.

Support Groups: Joining support groups or communities cantered around shared interests, hobbies, or personal struggles can provide a sense of belonging and understanding. These groups offer opportunities to connect with others who may be going through similar experiences and can provide support, empathy, and guidance.

Trusted Friends and Family: Reach out to trusted friends and family members who can offer a listening ear, companionship, and understanding. Share your feelings and experiences with them, and lean on their support during times of solitude and loneliness. Engaging in meaningful conversations and activities with loved ones can foster a sense of connection and belonging.

Online Communities: Connect with like-minded individuals through online communities, forums, or social media groups. These platforms can be a source of support, inspiration, and connection with people who share similar interests, passions, or experiences.

Volunteering and Giving Back: Engaging in volunteer work or community service allows you to connect with others while making a positive impact. By giving back to your community, you can foster a sense of connection, purpose, and fulfilment.

Engage in Social Activities: Participate in social activities and events that align with your interests and passions. This can include joining clubs, organizations, or hobby groups where you can meet new people who share similar interests.

Practice Active Listening: When engaging in conversations with others, practice active listening by being fully present and attentive. Show genuine interest in what others have to say, and validate their experiences and emotions. Building deep and meaningful connections with others requires active engagement and empathy.

Initiate Meaningful Conversations: Take the initiative to initiate meaningful conversations with others. Share your thoughts, ideas, and experiences openly, and encourage others to do the same. Engaging in deep and meaningful conversations can create a sense of connection and understanding.

Cultivate Empathy and Compassion: Develop empathy and compassion towards others. Seek to understand their perspectives, struggles, and joys. By fostering empathy, you can build stronger connections with others and create a supportive and nurturing environment.

Practice Vulnerability: Allow yourself to be vulnerable in your interactions with others. Share your authentic self, including your fears, hopes, and dreams. This openness can create deeper and more meaningful connections based on genuine understanding and acceptance.

Remember, seeking support and connection is a courageous step in overcoming loneliness and embracing solitude. It's important to surround yourself with individuals who uplift and support you on your journey. Building meaningful connections takes time and effort, but the rewards are invaluable in fostering a sense of belonging and fulfilment.

BALANCING SOLITUDE AND SOCIAL INTERACTION

Finding a harmonious balance between solitude and social engagement, understanding when to seek solitude for personal growth and rejuvenation, and when to reach out to others for connection and companionship.

Balancing solitude and social interaction is crucial for maintaining overall well-being and finding harmony in life. Here are some strategies for finding a balance between these two-

Self-Awareness: Develop self-awareness and tune into your needs and preferences. Pay attention to how you feel after periods of solitude and social interaction. Notice when you start to feel drained or overwhelmed and when you feel rejuvenated and fulfilled. This self-awareness will guide you in finding the right balance.

Intentional Solitude: Schedule intentional periods of solitude for self-reflection, introspection, and personal growth. Create a space and time for yourself to recharge, pursue your passions, and engage in activities that bring you joy and fulfilment. Use solitude as an opportunity for self-care and self-discovery.

Set Boundaries: Establish clear boundaries in your social interactions. Learn to say no when you need time for yourself and recognize when it's time to prioritize solitude. Communicate your needs to others and express your desire for alone time without feeling guilty or obligated.

Mindful Social Engagement: When you engage in social interactions, practice mindfulness. Be fully present and engaged in the moment, and choose connections that align with your values and bring you joy. Surround yourself with people who support and uplift you, and engage in activities that foster meaningful connections.

Quality over Quantity: Focus on the quality of your social interactions rather than the quantity. Seek out deep and meaningful connections rather than superficial ones. Prioritize relationships that nourish your soul and bring genuine companionship and understanding.

Flexibility and Adaptability: Be flexible and adaptable in your approach to solitude and social interaction. Recognize that your needs may vary at different stages of life or in different situations. Allow yourself the freedom to adjust and find a balance that works for you in each moment.

Regular Check-ins: Regularly check in with yourself to assess your energy levels, emotional well-being, and overall satisfaction with the balance between solitude and social interaction. Be open to making adjustments and modifications as needed to ensure your needs are being met.

Seek Variety: Incorporate a variety of social activities and experiences into your life. Engage in group activities, one-on-one interactions, and larger social gatherings. Explore different settings and environments that resonate with you and provide opportunities for connection and growth.

Listen to Your Intuition: Trust your intuition when it comes to finding the right balance between solitude and social interaction. Your inner voice will guide you in determining when it's time to seek solitude for personal rejuvenation and when it's time to reach out to others for connection and companionship.

Remember, finding a balance between solitude and social interaction is a personal journey. It may require some experimentation and adjustments to discover what works best for you. Embrace the ebb and flow of your needs and honour the importance of both solitude and social connection in your life.

TRANSCENDING LONELINESS THROUGH SERVICE AND CONTRIBUTION

Exploring the power of giving back to others, volunteering, and contributing to our communities as a way to combat loneliness and find a sense of purpose and fulfilment.

Transcending loneliness through service and contribution can be a transformative experience that not only benefits others but also helps us combat feelings of isolation and find a deeper sense of purpose and fulfilment. Here are some key points to consider-

Connection through Service: Engaging in acts of service and giving back to others can create meaningful connections and a sense of belonging. When we focus on the needs of others, we shift our attention away from our feelings of loneliness and cultivate a sense of interconnectedness with the community around us.

Finding Purpose: Serving others can provide a sense of purpose and meaning in life. By using our skills, talents, and resources to make a positive impact, we tap into a deeper sense of fulfilment and satisfaction. Contributing to something greater than ourselves gives us a sense of purpose and helps us see the value we bring to the world.

Building Relationships: Volunteering and engaging in service-oriented activities provide opportunities to meet new people and build meaningful relationships. Working alongside others who share similar values and goals can foster a sense of camaraderie and create lasting connections. These relationships can offer support, understanding, and companionship, helping to alleviate feelings of loneliness.

Perspective Shift: Serving others can help shift our perspective and broaden our worldview. It reminds us of the interconnectedness of humanity and the shared struggles and joys we all experience. This broader perspective can reduce feelings of isolation and remind us that we are part of a larger community.

Self-Reflection and Gratitude: Engaging in service allows for self-reflection and gratitude. As we help others, we gain a greater appreciation for our blessings and develop a sense of gratitude for what we have. This shift in perspective can bring us closer to others and cultivate a sense of contentment and fulfilment.

Engaging in Meaningful Activities: Look for volunteer opportunities or service activities that align with your passions and interests. Engaging in activities that you are genuinely passionate about will bring a greater sense of fulfilment and enjoyment. Whether it's working with a particular cause, supporting a local organization, or sharing your skills and expertise, find ways to contribute that resonate with you personally.

Starting Small: You don't have to commit to large-scale projects or time-consuming endeavours right away. Start small by finding small acts of kindness you can do each day or explore local volunteering opportunities. Even simple gestures like offering a helping hand to a neighbour, volunteering at a local shelter, or participating in community events can make a meaningful difference.

Regular Engagement: Make service and contribution a regular part of your life. Consider setting aside dedicated time each week or month to engage in acts of service. Consistency in giving back allows for deeper connections, a greater sense of purpose, and a continuous source of fulfilment.

Remember, the act of giving back is not only beneficial to those you serve but also to yourself. By transcending loneliness through service and contribution, you can create a positive ripple effect in your life and the lives of others, finding connection, purpose, and fulfilment along the way.

Sustaining Solitude and Connection:

Developing strategies for maintaining a healthy balance between solitude and meaningful connections over time, recognizing that both are essential for our overall well-being.

Maintaining a healthy balance between solitude and meaningful connections is crucial for our overall well-being. Here are some strategies to help sustain solitude and connection in a harmonious way-

Self-Awareness: Cultivate self-awareness to understand your needs and preferences when it comes to solitude and social interaction. Pay attention to how you feel after spending time alone or with others. Recognize the signs of when you need solitude for rejuvenation or when you crave social connection for companionship.

Intentional Time Management: Create a balance by consciously allocating time for solitude and social engagement. Prioritize both in your schedule and ensure that you have dedicated periods for personal reflection and self-care, as well as opportunities for meaningful interactions with others.

Mindful Socializing: When engaging in social activities, be present and fully engaged. Practice active listening, empathy, and genuine interest in others. This can help you create deeper connections and make the most of your social interactions, enhancing the quality of your relationships.

Honouring Boundaries: Establish and communicate your boundaries to others regarding your need for solitude and personal space. Let your loved ones know when you require time alone and express your needs respectfully. By setting boundaries, you can protect your alone time without feeling guilty or overwhelmed.

Selective Socializing: Choose social activities and connections that align with your values and interests. Surround yourself with people who uplift and support you, and engage in activities that bring you joy and fulfilment. This will ensure that your social interactions are meaningful and enjoyable, rather than draining or superficial.

Self-Care in Solitude: Use your solitude as a time for self-care and self-reflection. Engage in activities that nourish your mind, body, and soul, such as meditation, journaling, pursuing hobbies, or simply enjoying quiet moments of relaxation. This will help you recharge and maintain a healthy sense of self.

Cultivating Meaningful Connections: Seek out and nurture relationships that provide depth and meaning. Surround yourself with individuals who understand and respect your need for solitude and who appreciate the value of authentic connections. Invest your time and energy in relationships that bring fulfilment and mutual growth.

Flexibility and Adaptability: Recognize that the balance between solitude and connection may shift depending on your circumstances and life events. Be open to adjusting your routines and priorities as needed, while staying attuned to your well-being.

Regular Reflection: Periodically reflect on your experiences with solitude and social connection. Assess how well you are maintaining the balance and adjust your approach if necessary. Regular self-reflection will help you stay attuned to your needs and make necessary adjustments to sustain a healthy equilibrium.

Remember, finding a sustainable balance between solitude and connection is a personal journey. It may take time to discover what works best for you.

By prioritizing self-awareness, setting boundaries, nurturing meaningful connections, and honouring your needs, you can create a balanced and fulfilling life that embraces both solitude and connection.

PART SEVEN

Navigating Societal Pressures and Expectations

"Do not conform to the pattern of this world, but be transformed by the renewing of your mind." - Romans 12:2

In a world filled with expectations, norms, and societal pressures, it can be challenging to stay true to ourselves and live authentically. The quote from Romans 12:2 reminds us not to conform to the patterns of this world but instead to be transformed by renewing our minds. It speaks to the power of breaking free from societal molds and finding our paths, guided by our values, passions, and inner truths.

Navigating societal pressures and expectations requires courage, self-reflection, and a willingness to challenge the status quo. It means questioning the narratives that define what success, happiness, and fulfilment should look like, and instead, embracing a personal journey of self-discovery and growth.

In this exploration, we will delve into various sub-topics that shed light on the intricacies of navigating societal pressures and expectations. We will discuss the importance of understanding these pressures, challenging conformity, and redefining our definitions of success and happiness. We will explore the significance of embracing our individuality, nurturing self-confidence, and setting boundaries to protect our authenticity and well-being.

Moreover, we will uncover the value of finding supportive communities, both offline and online, that foster acceptance, validation, and encouragement outside of mainstream societal narratives. We will also emphasize the importance of unleashing our personal potential, pursuing our passions, and inspiring social change by living as examples of authenticity and breaking down societal barriers.

By engaging in this journey of self-discovery and self-empowerment, we can navigate societal pressures and expectations with resilience and grace. Together, let us embark on a transformative exploration of embracing our true selves, cultivating self-worth, and finding fulfilment on our terms.

UNDERSTANDING SOCIETAL PRESSURES

Examining the pervasive influence of societal norms, expectations, and cultural narratives that shape our beliefs, choices, and sense of self.

Societal pressures have a profound impact on our lives, shaping our thoughts, behaviours, and aspirations. From an early age, we are exposed to societal norms, expectations, and cultural narratives that dictate how we should look, act, and live our lives. These pressures can come from various sources such as family, education, media, and peer groups, and they often create a standard against which we measure our worth and success.

In this sub-topic, we will delve into the concept of societal pressures and examine their pervasive influence on our lives. We will explore the messages we receive about beauty standards, career paths, relationships, and other aspects of our lives, and how they can shape our beliefs and choices. By understanding these pressures, we can become more aware of their impact on our thoughts and behaviours, and begin to question their validity and relevance to our individual journeys.

We will also discuss the psychological and emotional consequences of succumbing to societal pressures, such as feelings of inadequacy, self-doubt, and the erosion of our authentic selves. By examining these effects, we can gain insight into the importance of breaking free from societal molds and discovering our unique paths.

Moreover, we will explore the intersectionality of

societal pressures, recognizing that different individuals may experience varying degrees and types of pressures based on factors such as gender, race, ethnicity, socioeconomic status, and more. By acknowledging these intersections, we can deepen our understanding of how societal pressures can impact different groups and work towards fostering inclusivity and equality.

Through this exploration, we aim to empower individuals to question and challenge societal pressures, encouraging them to define their values, beliefs, and sense of self-worth. By recognizing the influence of societal norms and expectations, we can begin to shape our personal narratives, embrace our authentic selves, and navigate a path that aligns with our true values and aspirations. Together, let us embark on a journey of self-discovery and liberation from societal pressures, ultimately transforming our minds and embracing a life of authenticity and fulfilment.

CHALLENGING CONFORMITY

Embracing the call to resist conformity and questioning the patterns of the world in order to cultivate our authentic identities and live in alignment with our values.

In a world that often encourages conformity, there is a profound call to resist and challenge the patterns that surround us. The quote from Romans 12:2 reminds us not to conform to the pattern of this world but to be transformed by the renewing of our minds. It urges us to break free from the expectations and norms imposed upon us and instead embrace our authentic identities.

In this sub-topic, we will explore the concept of challenging conformity and the importance of embracing our uniqueness. We will discuss the societal pressures that push us towards conformity, whether it be conforming to societal expectations, cultural norms, or even the opinions of others. By understanding these pressures, we can begin to question their validity and consider the impact they have on our sense of self and personal growth.

We will dig further into the power of self-discovery and self-reflection as tools to uncover our true identities and values. Through introspection and mindful observation, we can gain clarity on what truly resonates with us and aligns with our authentic selves. This process allows us to challenge the patterns of the world and instead forge our customized paths.

Additionally, we will explore the courage and resilience required to resist conformity. It can be challenging to go against the grain, to break free from societal expectations and follow our paths. However, by embracing our uniqueness and living in alignment with our values, we create the opportunity for personal growth, fulfilment, and a deep sense of purpose.

We will also discuss the role of community and support in challenging conformity. Surrounding ourselves with individuals who uplift and affirm our authentic selves can provide the encouragement and strength needed to stay true to our values and resist societal pressures. Together, we can create spaces that celebrate individuality and foster acceptance and inclusion.

By embracing the call to resist conformity, we open ourselves up to a transformative journey of self-discovery and personal growth. We challenge the patterns of the world and create space for our authentic identities to flourish. In doing so, we inspire others to do the same, fostering a culture of acceptance, diversity, and empowerment. Let us embark on this journey together, breaking free from conformity and embracing the beautiful tapestry of our individuality.

REDEFINING SUCCESS AND HAPPINESS

Exploring alternative definitions of success and happiness that go beyond societal benchmarks, allowing individuals to create their personal paths and find fulfilment on their terms.

In a society that often measures success and happiness based on external benchmarks, there is a need to redefine these concepts and discover our definitions that resonate with our true selves. The quote from Romans 12:2 encourages us to be transformed by the renewing of our minds, challenging us to redefine success and happiness on our terms.

In this sub-topic, we will delve into the exploration of alternative definitions of success and happiness. We will examine how societal pressures and expectations can influence our perception of these concepts, leading us to chase external validations and conform to predetermined standards. By understanding these influences, we can begin to question their validity and embark on a journey of self-discovery to define success and happiness based on our unique values and aspirations.

We will explore the notion that success goes beyond traditional markers such as wealth, status, or career achievements. Instead, we will delve into the idea that success can be found in personal growth, meaningful relationships, and the pursuit of our passions and purpose. By aligning our definition of success with our authentic selves, we can cultivate a sense of fulfilment and satisfaction that resonates deeply within us.

Similarly, we will challenge the notion that happiness is solely derived from external circumstances or material possessions. We will explore the importance of inner contentment, gratitude, and self-acceptance in cultivating genuine happiness. By shifting our focus inward and nurturing our mental and emotional well-being, we can discover a deeper sense of joy and fulfilment that transcends fleeting external circumstances.

Throughout this exploration, we will emphasize the significance of creating our paths and embracing our individual journeys. Each person's definition of success and happiness will be unique, reflecting their values, passions, and personal growth aspirations. By redefining these concepts on our terms, we empower ourselves to live authentically and make choices that align with our true desires and values.

We will also discuss the potential challenges and resistance that may arise when redefining success and happiness. Societal pressures and ingrained beliefs can create obstacles on this journey, requiring courage and resilience to overcome. However, by embracing our individual paths and staying true to our authentic selves, we can pave the way for personal fulfilment and a deep sense of purpose.

Together, let us embark on the journey of redefining success and happiness, challenging societal benchmarks, and creating our definitions that align with our authentic selves. By doing so, we open the door to a more fulfilling and meaningful existence, embracing a sense of purpose and joy that goes beyond external validations.

EMBRACING INDIVIDUALITY

Celebrating the uniqueness of each person and fostering self-acceptance, self-love, and self-expression in the face of societal pressures to fit into predefined molds.

In a world that often emphasizes conformity and fitting into predefined molds, embracing our individuality becomes an act of courage and self-empowerment. The quote from Romans 12:2 reminds us not to conform to the pattern of this world but to be transformed by renewing our minds. In this sub-topic, we will explore the importance of embracing individuality and celebrating the uniqueness of each person.

We live in a society that often imposes societal norms, expectations, and standards upon us, influencing the way we think, behave, and perceive ourselves. These pressures can create a sense of self-doubt, limiting our ability to fully express our authentic selves. However, by embracing individuality, we empower ourselves to break free from these constraints and live in alignment with our true identities.

Self-acceptance involves acknowledging and

honouring our authentic selves, cultivating a deep sense of love and compassion for who we are. By embracing our individuality, we foster a positive relationship with ourselves, promoting self-confidence and self-worth.

We will explore the significance of self-expression in embracing individuality. Each person possesses unique talents, passions, and perspectives that contribute to the rich tapestry of human diversity. By expressing ourselves authentically, whether through art, creativity, communication, or personal style, we celebrate our individuality and invite others to do the same. In doing so, we create spaces for self-expression that inspire and uplift both ourselves and those around us.

Throughout this exploration, we will confront the societal pressures to conform and fit into predefined molds. We will discuss the challenges that arise when embracing individuality, including potential judgment, criticism, or feelings of isolation. However, we will also highlight the transformative power of staying true to ourselves, as it fosters a deep sense of fulfilment, belonging, and inner harmony.

Together, we will celebrate the uniqueness of each

individual, recognizing that our differences contribute to the beauty and diversity of the human experience. By embracing individuality, we break free from the limitations imposed by societal expectations and pave the way for self-discovery, personal growth, and the realization of our full potential. Let us embark on this journey of self-acceptance, self-love, and self-expression, embracing our individuality with confidence and authenticity.

CULTIVATING A POSITIVE MINDSET

Developing a resilient mindset that is immune to external judgments and focuses on self-worth, personal growth, and embracing opportunities for learning and transformation.

In the face of societal pressures and expectations, cultivating a positive mindset becomes essential to navigate the challenges and embrace our individuality. The quote from Romans 12:2 encourages us to be transformed by the renewing of our minds, emphasizing the power of our thoughts and beliefs in shaping our experiences and perceptions. In this sub-topic, we will explore the importance of developing a positive mindset that is immune to external judgments and focuses on self-worth, personal growth, and embracing opportunities for learning and transformation.

A positive mindset involves cultivating a mental attitude that seeks the good in ourselves and others, reframing challenges as opportunities, and embracing a growth-oriented perspective. It starts with recognizing and challenging negative self-talk, self-limiting beliefs, and the influence of societal judgments. By consciously replacing negative thoughts with positive affirmations, we can shift our mindset and create a foundation of self-worth and self-empowerment.

Cultivating self-worth involves recognizing our unique strengths, talents, and qualities, and acknowledging that we are deserving of love, respect, and success simply because we exist. By anchoring our self-worth internally, we become less reliant on external validation and more resilient in the face of societal pressures.

A positive mindset also embraces personal growth and sees challenges as opportunities for learning and transformation. Instead of viewing setbacks or failures as indicators of inadequacy, we can reframe them as stepping stones on the path to growth and improvement. By embracing a growth-oriented perspective, we shift our focus from seeking

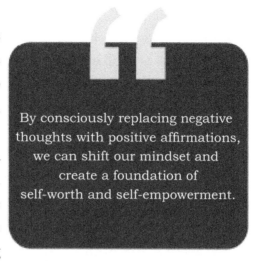

By consciously replacing negative thoughts with positive affirmations, we can shift our mindset and create a foundation of self-worth and self-empowerment.

perfection to valuing progress, resilience, and the lessons learned along the way.

Throughout this exploration, we will discuss techniques for cultivating a positive mindset, such as practicing gratitude, visualization, mindfulness, and self-compassion. These practices can help us rewire our brains to focus on the positive, build resilience, and develop a strong sense of self-belief. By cultivating a positive mindset, we empower ourselves to overcome societal pressures and embrace our individuality with confidence. We create a foundation of self-worth, resilience, and personal growth that enables us to navigate the challenges and uncertainties of life with grace and optimism. Together, let us embark on the journey of cultivating a positive mindset, transforming our thoughts, and embracing the power of self-belief and personal growth.

NURTURING SELF-CONFIDENCE

Building a strong sense of self-confidence and self-belief that empowers individuals to make choices that align with their authentic selves, even in the face of societal scrutiny.

Nurturing self-confidence is a crucial aspect of navigating societal pressures and expectations. The quote from Romans 12:2 reminds us not to conform to the pattern of this world, but rather to be transformed by renewing our minds. It emphasizes the importance of building a strong sense of self-confidence and self-belief that empowers individuals to make choices that align with their authentic selves, even in the face of societal scrutiny.

Self-confidence is the belief in one's own abilities, worth, and value. It is an inner strength that allows individuals to trust themselves, their judgment, and their unique qualities. When we have a healthy level of self-confidence, we are more likely to make decisions based on our values and aspirations rather than seeking validation or approval from others.

Building self-confidence involves a combination of self-awareness, self-acceptance, and self-empowerment. It starts with developing a deep understanding of ourselves, our strengths, and our areas for growth. By embracing our unique qualities and recognizing our inherent worth, we can cultivate a positive self-image that serves as the foundation for self-confidence.

Self-acceptance is another key component of nurturing self-confidence. It involves embracing and loving ourselves unconditionally, including our perceived flaws and imperfections. When we accept ourselves as we are, we free ourselves from the burden of striving for perfection or conforming to societal expectations. This allows us to authentically express ourselves and make choices that are aligned with our true desires and values.

To nurture self-confidence, it is important to cultivate self-empowerment. This involves setting and achieving goals, facing challenges, and stepping outside of our comfort zones. Each small accomplishment builds upon the previous ones, gradually strengthening our belief in our abilities and expanding our comfort zone. By taking risks and challenging ourselves, we prove to ourselves that we are capable and resilient.

Practicing self-compassion is also vital in nurturing self-confidence. It involves treating ourselves with kindness, understanding, and forgiveness, especially when we face setbacks or make mistakes. By cultivating self-compassion, we learn to be gentle with ourselves and recognize that failure or criticism does not define our worth or abilities. Instead, we see them as opportunities for growth and learning.

By nurturing self-confidence, we empower ourselves to navigate societal pressures and expectations with authenticity and resilience. We develop the courage to follow our path, make choices that align with our

> "When we accept ourselves as we are, we free ourselves from the burden of striving for perfection or conforming to societal expectations.

values and aspirations, and embrace our uniqueness. Together, let us embark on a journey of self-discovery and self-empowerment, building a strong sense of self-confidence that allows us to shine brightly and make a positive impact in the world.

FINDING SUPPORTIVE COMMUNITIES

Seeking out and connecting with communities, groups, or individuals who share similar values and beliefs, providing encouragement, validation, and a sense of belonging outside of mainstream societal narratives.

Finding supportive communities is a valuable aspect of navigating societal pressures and expectations. As we strive to live authentically and embrace our unique identities, it is essential to connect with others who share similar values and beliefs. The quote from Romans 12:2 encourages us not to conform to the pattern of this world but to be transformed by renewing our minds. Seeking out and connecting with supportive communities can help us in this transformation.

Supportive communities provide a sense of

belonging and underst anding that is often lacking in mainstream societal narratives. These communities can be found in various forms, such as interest-based groups,

> When we connect with supportive communities, we surround ourselves with like-minded individuals who can relate to our struggles, aspirations, and values.

cultural or identity-based communities, spiritual or religious organizations, or online platforms. They offer spaces where individuals can express themselves freely, share their experiences, and find support and validation.

When we connect with supportive communities, we surround ourselves with like-minded individuals who can relate to our struggles, aspirations, and values. We no longer feel isolated or misunderstood but instead find solace and encouragement in the company of others who share our perspectives. These communities can offer valuable guidance, insights, and inspiration as we navigate the challenges of resisting societal pressures.

Supportive communities can also serve as platforms for personal growth and empowerment. Through engaging with others who are on similar paths, we can learn from their experiences, gain new perspectives, and acquire valuable skills and knowledge. These communities often foster an atmosphere of collaboration and mutual support, encouraging individuals to explore their potential, set and achieve goals, and challenge themselves to grow.

In seeking out supportive communities, it is important to be intentional and discerning. Consider your values, interests, and goals, and seek communities that align with them. Look for spaces that prioritize inclusivity, respect, and empathy, where diverse voices and experiences are valued and celebrated. Engage in activities, events, or conversations that resonate with you and allow you to connect with others authentically.

Online platforms and social media can also be valuable resources for finding supportive communities, as they provide opportunities to connect with individuals from all over the world who share similar interests or values. However, it is crucial to approach online communities with discernment and ensure that they maintain a positive and respectful environment.

By finding supportive communities, we create a network of individuals who uplift and validate our journey. We can seek advice, share our achievements and struggles, and find solace in knowing that we are not alone in challenging societal expectations. These communities can offer the support and encouragement needed to stay true to ourselves, pursue our passions, and find fulfilment beyond the confines of mainstream narratives.

In the following pages, we will explore strategies for finding and engaging with supportive communities, including practical tips for seeking out like-minded individuals, participating in community activities, and contributing to the growth and well-being of the community. Together, let us embark on a journey of connection and belonging, finding strength and inspiration in the power of supportive communities as we navigate societal pressures and expectations.

UNLEASHING PERSONAL POTENTIAL

Embracing personal growth, self-discovery, and the

pursuit of passions and talents as a means of transcending societal limitations and living a purpose-driven life.

Unleashing personal potential is an empowering journey that allows individuals to transcend societal limitations and live a purpose-driven life. In the quote from Romans 12:2, we are encouraged to be transformed by the renewing of our minds, signalling the importance of personal growth, self-discovery, and the pursuit of our passions and talents.

Societal pressures and expectations often impose limitations on individuals, dictating what is considered successful or acceptable. However, by embracing personal growth, we challenge these limitations and embark on a path of self-discovery and self-actualization. This journey involves recognizing and unleashing our unique potential, talents, and passions.

Personal growth involves an ongoing process of self-improvement, learning, and development. It requires a willingness to step outside of our comfort zones, embrace new experiences, and continuously expand our knowledge and skills. Through personal growth, we gain a deeper understanding of ourselves, our values, and our aspirations.

Self-discovery is an essential aspect of unleashing personal potential. It involves exploring our inner world, examining our beliefs, strengths, weaknesses, and passions. By engaging in introspection and reflection, we uncover our authentic selves and gain clarity about what truly resonates with us. Self-discovery allows us to align our actions and choices with our core values and aspirations, rather than conforming to external expectations.

The pursuit of passions and talents plays a significant role in unleashing personal potential. When we engage in activities and endeavours that ignite our enthusiasm and bring us joy, we tap into our innate abilities and creativity. Passion fuels our motivation and commitment, enabling us to excel and make meaningful contributions in our chosen fields.

By unleashing personal potential, we transcend societal limitations and redefine success on our terms. We no longer measure our worth solely by external achievements or societal standards.

Instead, we embrace a purpose-driven life, where success is defined by the fulfilment and impact we experience as we live in alignment with our passions, values, and talents.

Embracing personal growth, self-discovery, and the pursuit of passions and talents requires courage, resilience, and a belief in our potential. It involves challenging societal norms, stepping away from comparison and competition, and cultivating a deep sense of self-awareness and self-confidence. It is a continuous journey that requires dedication, perseverance, and a commitment to lifelong learning and development.

In the following chapters, we will delve deeper into strategies and practices that can support us in unleashing our personal potential. We will explore techniques for self-discovery, methods for cultivating personal growth, and ways to

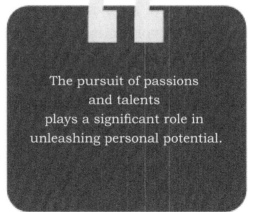

The pursuit of passions and talents plays a significant role in unleashing personal potential.

nurture and pursue our passions and talents. Together, let us embark on a transformative journey of unleashing our personal potential, transcending societal limitations, and living a purpose-driven life that is aligned with our true selves.

INSPIRING SOCIAL CHANGE

Using personal experiences, stories, and actions to challenge societal norms, broaden perspectives, and advocate for a more inclusive and accepting society that celebrates individuality and diverse paths to fulfilment.

Inspiring social change is a powerful way to challenge societal norms, broaden perspectives, and advocate for a more inclusive and accepting society. It involves using our personal experiences, stories, and actions to create a positive impact and pave the way for a world that celebrates individuality and diverse paths to fulfilment.

Every person's journey is unique, and by sharing our personal experiences, we can shed light on different perspectives and challenge the status quo. Sharing our stories allows us to connect with others, fostering empathy, understanding, and a sense of common humanity. It helps to break down barriers and dismantle stereotypes, showing that there is no one-size-fits-all approach to happiness, success, or fulfilment. Our personal experiences can serve as powerful catalysts for change. By speaking up, sharing our struggles, triumphs, and lessons learned, we encourage others to do the same. Through authenticity and vulnerability, we create spaces for dialogue and open the door for meaningful conversations that can challenge deeply ingrained societal norms.

In addition to sharing personal experiences, taking action is essential in inspiring social change. It involves actively engaging in initiatives, projects, or movements that promote inclusivity, equality, and acceptance. Whether it's volunteering for a cause,

> Through authenticity and vulnerability, we create spaces for dialogue and open the door for meaningful conversations that can challenge deeply ingrained societal norms.

advocating for marginalized communities, or participating in grassroots movements, our actions have the potential to create ripples of change that extend far beyond ourselves.

One of the most effective ways to inspire social change is by being a role model. By living our lives authentically and unapologetically, we become beacons of possibility, showing others that it is indeed possible to forge their paths, pursue their passions, and live fulfilling lives that align with their values. Our actions can inspire and empower others to challenge societal norms and embrace their true selves.

In the pursuit of social change, it's important to recognize that progress may take time and effort. It requires resilience, patience, and a commitment to continuous learning and growth. We may face resistance, criticism, or setbacks along the way, but by staying true to our values and remaining steadfast in our vision, we can create lasting change.

As we embark on the journey of inspiring social change, let us remember that our individual actions and stories have the power to ignite collective transformation. By challenging societal norms, broadening perspectives, and advocating for inclusivity and acceptance, we can contribute to the creation of a more compassionate, equitable, and diverse world.

PART EIGHT

Thriving in Singleness: Mind, Body, and Spirit

"Or do you not know that your body is a temple of the Holy Spirit within you, whom you have from God? You are not your own." -
1 Corinthians 6:19

In a world that often emphasizes the importance of romantic relationships, it can be empowering and liberating to embrace the journey of thriving in singleness. The quote from 1 Corinthians 6:19 reminds us that our bodies are temples of the Holy Spirit and that we are not defined solely by our relationship status. Thriving in singleness encompasses nurturing our mind, body, and spirit to cultivate a fulfilling and purposeful life.

Thriving in singleness is an opportunity for self-discovery, personal growth, and self-love. It is a time to focus on developing a deep understanding of oneself, exploring passions and interests, and nurturing meaningful connections with others. It is a time to recognize the inherent worth and value within us, independent of any romantic partnership.

In this journey of thriving in singleness, we explore how to cultivate a healthy and positive mindset, prioritize self-care, and embrace our individuality. It involves nurturing our mental well-being, fostering a sense of physical vitality, and nourishing our spiritual connection. Thriving in singleness encourages us to build strong foundations within ourselves, establishing a sense of wholeness and contentment that goes beyond our relationship status.

This Part delves into the various aspects of thriving in singleness—mind, body, and spirit. We will explore strategies for cultivating self-confidence, setting and achieving personal goals, and embracing opportunities for personal growth and self-discovery. We will discuss the importance of self-care, healthy lifestyle choices, and practices that promote physical well-being. Additionally, we will delve into nurturing our spiritual connection, finding purpose and meaning in our lives, and developing a deeper relationship with God.

Thriving in singleness is not about negating the desire for romantic love or disregarding the importance of relationships. Instead, it is an invitation to recognize the inherent value in being single, to celebrate the joys and freedoms that come with this season of life, and to create a fulfilling and purpose-driven life regardless of relationship status.

EMBRACING SINGLENESS
Understanding the Value and Significance of the Single Season

In a society that often romanticizes romantic relationships and places a high value on being coupled up, it is essential to recognize and appreciate the unique value and significance of the single season. Embracing singleness allows individuals to focus on personal growth, self-discovery, and building a strong foundation for future relationships, if desired. By reframing societal perceptions and understanding the benefits of being single, we can empower ourselves and others to embrace this season of life.

CHALLENGING SOCIETAL PERCEPTIONS

a. Addressing cultural expectations: Societal norms and cultural expectations often place undue pressure on individuals to be in relationships. By challenging these expectations, we can break free from the notion that being single is a failure or a temporary state.

b. Redefining success: Success should not be solely defined by one's relationship status. By valuing personal achievements, career growth, and individual happiness, we can broaden the definition of success beyond romantic partnerships.

OPPORTUNITIES FOR PERSONAL GROWTH

a. Self-reflection and introspection: The single season offers a unique opportunity for self-reflection and introspection. Without the distractions of a romantic relationship, individuals can explore their passions, interests, and values, fostering personal growth and self-awareness.

b. Pursuing personal goals and aspirations: Being single allows individuals to dedicate their time and energy to pursue personal goals and aspirations. Whether it's further education, career advancement, or travel, this period can be incredibly fruitful for personal development.

SELF-DISCOVERY AND BUILDING A STRONG FOUNDATION

a. Learning to love oneself: Embracing singleness provides a chance to develop a deep sense of self-love and self-acceptance. By prioritizing self-care, nurturing positive self-esteem, and exploring personal interests, individuals can cultivate a strong foundation for future relationships.

b. Building a support network: The single season allows for the cultivation of diverse relationships and friendships, which can serve as a crucial support network. These connections provide emotional support, companionship, and opportunities for personal growth.

EMBRACING INDEPENDENCE AND FREEDOM

a. Empowerment through independence: Singleness encourages individuals to become self-reliant and independent. This independence can lead to a greater sense of empowerment, self-confidence, and resilience.

b. Exploring new experiences: Being single opens doors to new experiences, such as trying new hobbies, exploring different communities, and traveling solo. These experiences foster personal growth, broaden perspectives, and create lifelong memories.

Embracing singleness is about recognizing the value and significance of this season of life. By reframing societal perceptions, focusing on personal growth and self-discovery, and embracing the opportunities for independence and freedom, individuals can find fulfilment and happiness in their single journey. It is a time to cultivate self-love, build a strong foundation, and create a meaningful life that can enhance future relationships or simply be cherished for its inherent worth.

SELF-ACCEPTANCE
Developing a Positive and Compassionate Relationship with Oneself

Self-acceptance is a fundamental aspect of personal well-being and happiness. It involves developing a positive and compassionate relationship with oneself, honouring personal needs, and fostering a strong sense of self-worth and contentment. By cultivating self-acceptance, individuals can embrace their strengths and weaknesses, overcome self-criticism, and live authentically, leading to a more fulfilling and satisfying life.

EMBRACING IMPERFECTIONS

a. Recognizing uniqueness: Self-acceptance begins with acknowledging that each person is unique, with their strengths, weaknesses, and experiences. Embrace your individuality and appreciate the qualities that make you who you are.

b. Letting go of perfectionism: Understand that perfection is an unattainable goal. Embracing imperfections allows for personal growth and learning from mistakes, fostering self-compassion and resilience.

NURTURING SELF-COMPASSION

a. Treating oneself with kindness: Cultivate a mindset of self-compassion by treating yourself with the same kindness and understanding you would offer a close friend. Be patient, forgiving, and supportive during challenging times.

b. Embracing self-care: Prioritize self-care practices that nourish your physical, emotional, and mental well-being. Take time for activities that bring you joy, relaxation, and rejuvenation.

HONOURING PERSONAL NEEDS

a. Setting boundaries: Understand and communicate your boundaries to protect your physical and emotional well-being. Learn to say no when necessary and prioritize activities that align with your values and needs.

b. Prioritizing self-care: Acknowledge and fulfil your basic needs, including proper nutrition, regular exercise, adequate rest, and maintaining a healthy work-life balance. Prioritizing self-care demonstrates self-respect and reinforces a positive self-image.

CULTIVATING SELF-WORTH AND AUTHENTICITY

a. Recognizing inherent value: Understand that your worth is not defined by external factors or achievements. Recognize your inherent value as a human being and embrace your strengths, talents, and unique qualities.

b. Living authentically: Be true to yourself and honour your values, passions, and interests. Living authentically promotes a sense of congruence and contentment, as you align your actions with your true self.

PRACTICING GRATITUDE AND MINDFULNESS

a. Gratitude for self: Cultivate a practice of gratitude, focusing on the positive aspects of yourself and your life. Celebrate your accomplishments, no matter how small, and appreciate the qualities that make you special.

b. Mindfulness for self-acceptance: Practice

mindfulness to cultivate awareness of your thoughts, emotions, and self-talk. By observing without judgment, you can recognize and challenge self-critical thoughts, promoting self-acceptance and inner peace.

Self-acceptance is a journey of embracing oneself with kindness, compassion, and authenticity. By nurturing self-acceptance, individuals can develop a positive and compassionate relationship with themselves, honour personal needs, and foster a strong sense of self-worth and contentment. Embracing imperfections, practicing self-compassion, setting boundaries, cultivating self-worth, and embracing gratitude and mindfulness are all essential steps toward a more fulfilling and contented life. Remember, self-acceptance is a lifelong process, and each step taken brings you closer to embracing your true self.

NURTURING MENTAL WELL-BEING

Strategies for Maintaining Mental Health and Cultivating Resilience in Singleness

Maintaining mental well-being is crucial for everyone, including those embracing the single season. Being single can bring about unique challenges and joys. By implementing strategies to manage stress, prioritize self-care, and cultivate a resilient mindset, individuals can nurture their mental health and embrace the full potential of their single journey.

PRIORITIZING SELF-CARE

a. Establishing a self-care routine: Create a routine that includes activities promoting relaxation, rejuvenation, and self-reflection. This may involve practices such as exercise, meditation, journaling, or engaging in hobbies that bring joy and fulfilment.

b. Setting boundaries: Protect your mental health by setting boundaries in relationships, work, and social engagements. Learn to say no when necessary and allocate time for rest and rejuvenation.

MANAGING STRESS

a. Stress management techniques: Explore stress management techniques that work for you, such as deep breathing exercises, mindfulness meditation, or engaging in creative outlets. These techniques can help reduce stress and promote a sense of calm and balance.

b. Time management: Organize your time effectively, prioritizing tasks and activities that align with your goals and values. Create a schedule that allows for both productivity and relaxation, minimizing the chances of feeling overwhelmed.

CULTIVATING RESILIENCE

a. Developing a growth mindset: Embrace challenges as opportunities for growth and learning. Adopt a growth mindset, focusing on solutions rather than dwelling on problems. Reframe setbacks as valuable experiences that contribute to personal development.

b. Building a support network: Surround yourself with supportive friends, family, or like-minded individuals who can provide encouragement and a listening ear. Seeking support when needed can help navigate the ups and downs of the single journey.

ENGAGING IN POSITIVE SELF-TALK AND AFFIRMATIONS

a. Practicing positive self-talk: Become aware of

your inner dialogue and challenge negative self-talk. Replace self-criticism with self-compassion and supportive, affirming statements. Remind yourself of your worth, strengths, and resilience.

b. Affirmations and mantras: Use positive affirmations and mantras to reinforce a resilient mindset and boost self-confidence. Repeat affirmations that resonate with you, such as "I am enough" or "I embrace the journey of self-discovery and growth."

EMBRACING JOY AND GRATITUDE

a. Fostering gratitude: Cultivate a gratitude practice to shift your focus towards the positive aspects of your life. Regularly acknowledge and appreciate the blessings, joys, and opportunities that come with being single.

b. Embracing joy and hobbies: Engage in activities that bring you joy, fulfilment, and a sense of purpose. Pursue hobbies, explore new interests, and create opportunities for fun and excitement in your single journey.

Nurturing mental well-being is essential for embracing the challenges and joys of singleness. By prioritizing self-care, managing stress, cultivating resilience, engaging in positive self-talk, and embracing joy and gratitude, individuals can maintain their mental health and navigate the single season with confidence and contentment. Remember that your mental well-being is a priority, and investing in yourself emotionally and mentally will enhance your overall quality of life during this transformative period.

PURSUING PERSONAL GROWTH AND DEVELOPMENT

Cultivating Fulfilment through Goal Setting, Passion Exploration, and Lifelong Learning

Personal growth and development are essential components of a fulfilling life, regardless of relationship status. Embracing singleness provides a unique opportunity to focus on self-discovery, set meaningful goals, explore passions, and invest in lifelong learning. By pursuing personal growth, individuals can cultivate fulfilment, expand their horizons, and create a purpose-driven life.

SETTING MEANINGFUL GOALS

a. Reflecting on values and aspirations: Take time to identify your core values, passions, and aspirations. Use them as a compass to set meaningful and authentic goals that align with who you are and what you want to achieve.

b. SMART goal setting: Employ the SMART (Specific, Measurable, Achievable, Relevant, Time-bound) framework to set clear and actionable goals. Break down larger goals into smaller, manageable steps to track progress and maintain motivation.

EXPLORING PASSIONS AND INTERESTS

a. Trying new activities: Embrace the freedom of singleness to explore new hobbies, interests, and experiences. Step out of your comfort zone and engage in activities that ignite your curiosity and bring you joy.

b. Cultivating existing passions: Deepen your involvement in activities that already inspire and energize you. Dedicate time to nurture and develop these passions, allowing them to contribute to your personal growth.

INVESTING IN LIFELONG LEARNING

a. Pursuing education and skill development: Take advantage of the wealth of educational resources available. Enrol in courses, workshops, or seminars to acquire new knowledge and skills that align with your interests and goals.

b. Reading and self-study: Engage in regular reading and self-study to expand your understanding of various subjects. Dive into books, articles, and online resources to broaden your perspectives and deepen your intellectual curiosity.

EMBRACING CHALLENGES AND LEARNING FROM SETBACKS

a. Stepping outside comfort zones: Growth often happens outside of comfort zones. Embrace challenges and embrace the opportunity to learn and develop resilience as you navigate unfamiliar territory.

b. Viewing setbacks as learning experiences: See setbacks as opportunities for growth and learning. Reframe failures as valuable lessons that contribute to personal development and propel you forward.

SEEKING PERSONAL DEVELOPMENT RESOURCES AND SUPPORT

a. Mentors and role models: Seek out mentors or role models who inspire you in your chosen areas of personal growth. Learn from their experiences, seek guidance, and leverage their insights to accelerate your development.

b. Supportive communities: Engage with supportive communities and networks that share similar interests and goals. Collaborate, exchange ideas, and find encouragement and accountability in like-minded individuals.

Pursuing personal growth and development is a transformative journey that can bring immense fulfilment during the single season. By setting meaningful goals, exploring passions, investing in lifelong learning, embracing challenges, and seeking support, individuals can cultivate a purpose-driven life and continuously evolve. Embrace the opportunities that singleness affords to discover your true potential, expand your horizons, and create a rich and meaningful life that aligns with your passions, values, and aspirations.

Remember, personal growth is a lifelong process, and each step taken brings you closer to becoming the best version of yourself.

NOURISHING PHYSICAL WELL-BEING

Promoting Vitality and Well-Being through Healthy Lifestyle Choices

Physical well-being is a cornerstone of overall health and vitality. Regardless of relationship status, prioritizing physical health is crucial for leading a fulfilling and balanced life. By understanding the importance of physical well-being and adopting healthy lifestyle choices, such as regular exercise, proper nutrition, and self-care practices, individuals can promote vitality, boost energy levels, and enhance their overall well-being.

RECOGNIZING THE IMPORTANCE OF PHYSICAL HEALTH

a. Holistic well-being: Understand that physical health is interconnected with mental and emotional well-being. Nurturing your body supports a positive mindset, enhances resilience, and improves overall quality of life.

b. Prevention and longevity: By taking care of your physical health, you reduce the risk of chronic diseases, enhance longevity, and improve your ability to engage fully in various aspects of life.

REGULAR EXERCISE AND MOVEMENT

a. Finding enjoyable activities: Engage in physical activities that you genuinely enjoy, such as walking, jogging, dancing, swimming, or practicing yoga. Choose activities that align with your interests and provide both physical and mental benefits.

b. Establishing a routine: Create a consistent exercise routine that incorporates a variety of activities, including cardiovascular exercises, strength training, and flexibility exercises. Aim for at least 150 minutes of moderate-intensity aerobic activity per week.

BALANCED NUTRITION

a. Prioritizing whole foods: Emphasize a balanced diet consisting of whole, nutrient-dense foods such as fruits, vegetables, whole grains, lean proteins, and healthy fats. Minimize processed foods, added sugars, and unhealthy fats.

b. Adequate hydration: Stay properly hydrated by consuming an adequate amount of water throughout the day. Water is essential for various bodily functions and supports overall health.

REST AND SLEEP

a. Prioritizing sleep: Establish a consistent sleep routine and aim for 7-9 hours of quality sleep each night. Create a soothing bedtime routine, optimize your sleep environment, and practice relaxation techniques to improve sleep quality.

b. Rest and recovery: Allow yourself regular periods of rest and relaxation. Incorporate breaks throughout the day, engage in stress-reducing activities, and prioritize activities that promote relaxation and rejuvenation.

SELF-CARE PRACTICES:

a. Stress management: Implement stress-management techniques such as deep breathing exercises, meditation, or engaging in activities that help you relax and unwind. Prioritize self-care practices that promote stress reduction and emotional well-being.

b. Mind-body connection: Cultivate a strong mind-body connection by incorporating practices like mindfulness, yoga, or tai chi. These practices promote physical and mental relaxation, improve flexibility and balance, and enhance overall well-being.

Nourishing physical well-being is essential for a balanced and fulfilling life, irrespective of relationship status. By recognizing the importance of physical health and adopting healthy lifestyle choices, including regular exercise, balanced nutrition, restful sleep, and self-care practices, individuals can enhance vitality, promote well-being, and optimize their overall quality of life. Remember, small and consistent changes in lifestyle can lead to significant improvements in physical health, providing a solid foundation for embracing the joys and challenges of life with vitality and energy.

EXPLORING SPIRITUALITY AND FAITH

Deepening the Connection, Finding Meaning, and Embracing Personal Growth and Fulfilment

Exploring spirituality and faith is a profound journey that can provide individuals with a deeper sense of meaning, purpose, and personal growth. Regardless of relationship status, embracing spirituality allows for a connection with something greater than oneself, deepening the relationship with God or the divine. By seeking a deeper spiritual connection, finding meaning in one's faith journey, and embracing spiritual practices, individuals can experience personal growth and fulfilment in their lives.

SEEKING A DEEPER CONNECTION

a. Reflection and introspection: Take time for self-reflection and introspection to explore your beliefs, values, and the role of spirituality in your life. Engage in activities that foster self-awareness and contemplation, such as journaling or meditation.

b. Prayer and meditation: Foster a deeper connection with God or the divine through prayer and meditation. Set aside dedicated time to engage in these practices, allowing for moments of silence, gratitude, and open communication.

FINDING MEANING AND PURPOSE

a. Exploring your faith tradition: Dive into the

teachings, scriptures, and traditions of your faith. Seek understanding and interpretation that resonates with you, and reflect on how these teachings can guide your life and provide meaning and purpose.

b. Connecting with a community: Engage with a supportive spiritual community or congregation that shares your beliefs. Participate in communal worship, study groups, or service activities that allow for connection, support, and the exploration of faith together.

EMBRACING SPIRITUAL PRACTICES

a. Rituals and ceremonies: Incorporate meaningful rituals and ceremonies into your spiritual practice. These may include lighting candles, reciting prayers or mantras, or participating in sacred ceremonies that align with your faith tradition.

b. Mindfulness and gratitude: Cultivate mindfulness and gratitude as spiritual practices. Practice being present in the moment, appreciate the beauty of the world around you, and express gratitude for blessings and experiences.

ENGAGING IN SERVICE AND COMPASSION

a. Acts of service: Embrace the opportunity to serve others, whether within your faith community or in the wider world. Engaging in acts of service and compassion allows for the embodiment of your faith and the expression of love and kindness towards others.

b. Practicing forgiveness and empathy: Foster forgiveness and empathy as integral aspects of your spiritual journey. Seek to understand others' perspectives, extend compassion, and practice forgiveness, both towards others and yourself.

INTEGRATING SPIRITUAL INSIGHTS INTO DAILY LIFE

a. Reflective practices: Integrate reflective practices into your daily life, such as daily affirmations, reading spiritual texts, or engaging in devotional practices. Allow these practices to inspire and guide your thoughts, actions, and decision-making.

b. Applying teachings in action: Live out the principles and teachings of your faith in your daily interactions and choices. Strive to align your behaviour with your spiritual beliefs, embodying love, compassion, integrity, and justice.

Exploring spirituality and faith is a transformative journey that can bring deep meaning, purpose, and personal growth. By seeking a deeper spiritual connection, finding meaning in your faith journey, and embracing spiritual practices, you can nurture your relationship with God or the divine and experience fulfilment in your life. Remember that spirituality is a deeply personal journey, and there are various paths to explore. Embrace the opportunity to delve into your faith, connect with a supportive community, and integrate spiritual insights into your daily life. Through this exploration, you can embark on a transformative and enriching spiritual journey, fostering personal growth and finding greater fulfilment in the single season and beyond.

EMBRACING INDEPENDENCE AND FREEDOM

Seizing Opportunities for Self-Discovery, Adventure, and Personal Fulfilment in Singleness

Singleness brings a unique sense of freedom and autonomy, offering individuals the opportunity to fully embrace independence and celebrate their individuality. By recognizing and appreciating the freedom that comes with being single, individuals can embark on a journey of self-discovery, seek new adventures, and find personal fulfilment. Embracing independence allows for the exploration of passions, the pursuit of personal growth, and the creation of a life that aligns with one's desires and aspirations.

CELEBRATING INDIVIDUALITY AND SELF-DISCOVERY

a. Embracing uniqueness: Recognize and celebrate your individuality. Embrace the freedom to be authentic and true to yourself, allowing your passions, interests, and personality to shine.

b. Self-exploration: Use this season of singleness as an opportunity for self-discovery. Engage in activities that allow you to better understand your strengths, weaknesses, values, and aspirations. Reflect on what brings you joy and fulfilment.

SEIZING OPPORTUNITIES FOR ADVENTURE

a. Exploring new horizons: Embrace the freedom to embark on new adventures and explore uncharted territories. Take advantage of opportunities to travel, try new experiences, and step outside of your comfort zone.

b. Solo adventures: Embrace the beauty of solo travel or engaging in activities independently. It allows for self-reliance, personal growth, and the opportunity to connect with new people and cultures on a deeper level.

PURSUING PERSONAL FULFILMENT

a. Setting personal goals: Identify your personal goals and aspirations. Use this time to focus on achieving them without compromising your desires and dreams. Define what fulfilment means to you and pursue it wholeheartedly.

b. Cultivating self-care and self-love: Prioritize self-care practices that nourish your physical, emotional, and spiritual well-being. Practice self-love and self-compassion, treating yourself with kindness and respect.

BUILDING A SUPPORTIVE NETWORK

a. Surrounding yourself with like-minded individuals: Seek out a supportive network of friends, mentors, and like-minded individuals who share similar values and aspirations. They can provide encouragement, inspiration, and companionship on your journey.

b. Engaging in community and social activities:
Participate in community events, organizations, or social groups that align with your interests and passions. Connect with others who share your enthusiasm and engage in meaningful conversations and activities.

EMBRACING INDEPENDENCE WITH GRATITUDE

a. Gratitude for the freedom: Cultivate a sense of gratitude for the freedom and autonomy that comes with singleness. Embrace the ability to make independent decisions, follow your path, and create a life that reflects your true self.

b. Embracing the present moment: Practice mindfulness and presence by savouring the present moment. Appreciate the opportunities and experiences that come your way and find joy in the journey of embracing your independence.

Embracing independence and freedom during the single season is a remarkable opportunity for self-discovery, adventure, and personal fulfilment. Celebrate your individuality, seize opportunities for new experiences and adventures, pursue personal goals, and build a supportive network. Embrace the freedom to create a life that aligns with your desires, passions, and aspirations. Embracing independence with gratitude allows you to fully embrace the joys and opportunities of singleness, leading to personal growth, fulfilment, and a deeper understanding of oneself. Celebrate this season of independence, and let it be a transformative and empowering chapter in your life.

THRIVING IN SINGLENESS IN A RELATIONSHIP-CENTRIC WORLD

Navigating Societal Pressures, Dispelling Myths, and Cultivating a Positive Mindset

In a society that often emphasizes romantic relationships, thriving in singleness can sometimes feel challenging. However, it is essential to recognize that being single is a valuable and fulfilling life choice. By navigating societal pressures, dispelling myths and misconceptions, and cultivating a positive mindset, individuals can embrace their single status and create a meaningful and empowered life.

UNDERSTANDING SOCIETAL PRESSURES

a. Recognizing societal narratives: Acknowledge the relationship-centric narratives prevalent in society. Understand that these narratives do not define your worth or happiness and that being single is a valid and fulfilling choice.

b. Challenging societal expectations: Challenge societal expectations that place undue pressure on being in a romantic relationship. Reframe your perspective and prioritize your well-being and personal growth.

DISPELLING MYTHS AND MISCONCEPTIONS

a. Embracing individual paths: Understand that there is no one-size-fits-all approach to relationships and happiness. Each individual has unique desires, goals, and timelines. Embrace the freedom to shape your path and define success on your terms.

b. Celebrating diverse forms of love: Recognize that love and connection can be found in various forms, including friendships, family relationships, and self-love. Embrace the richness of these connections and cherish the meaningful relationships in your life.

CULTIVATING A POSITIVE MINDSET

a. Embracing self-acceptance: Practice self-acceptance and embrace your single status as an opportunity for personal growth and self-discovery. Focus on your strengths, accomplishments, and the unique qualities that make you who you are.

b. Shifting focus to personal fulfilment: Redirect your focus from external validation through relationships to personal fulfilment. Engage in activities and pursue passions that bring you joy, growth, and a sense of purpose.

NURTURING SUPPORTIVE RELATIONSHIPS

a. Surrounding yourself with a supportive network: Cultivate a network of friends, family, and like-minded individuals who support and understand your choice to be single. Surround yourself with positive influences who celebrate your independence and personal growth.

b. Seeking community: Engage with communities or groups that share similar values and interests. Connect with others who appreciate and celebrate the single season, allowing for shared experiences and support.

PRACTICING SELF-CARE AND SELF-COMPASSION

a. Prioritizing self-care: Take care of your physical, emotional, and mental well-being through self-care practices. Engage in activities that rejuvenate and nourish your soul, such as exercise, mindfulness, hobbies, and pursuing personal interests.

b. Practicing self-compassion: Be kind and compassionate towards yourself. Acknowledge that being single is a valid choice and grant yourself the same love, care, and understanding that you would offer to others.

Thriving in singleness is about embracing your journey, challenging societal expectations, and cultivating a positive mindset. By navigating societal pressures, dispelling myths and misconceptions, and fostering a supportive network, individuals can create a fulfilling and empowered life. Embrace your single status with confidence and self-assurance, knowing that it is a valuable season for personal growth, self-discovery, and creating a life that aligns with your authentic self. Remember that your worth and happiness are not dependent on being in a romantic relationship, and you have the power to shape your narrative and thrive in the face of societal expectations.

EMBRACING THE JOURNEY

Finding Joy, Growth, and Transformation in the Season of Singleness

The journey of thriving in singleness is an ongoing process that presents individuals with unique opportunities for personal growth, self-discovery, and transformation. By recognizing and embracing the joys, challenges, and transformative experiences that come with this season of life, individuals can cultivate resilience, deepen self-awareness, and create a fulfilling and meaningful life.

EMBRACING THE JOYS OF SINGLENESS

a. Celebrating freedom and autonomy: Recognize the freedom and autonomy that singleness offers. Embrace the ability to make independent choices, pursue personal passions, and explore new opportunities without compromising your desires and aspirations.

b. Cultivating self-love and self-care: Use this season to prioritize self-love and self-care. Engage in activities that nurture your physical, emotional, and spiritual well-being, and develop a deep sense of compassion and appreciation for yourself.

NAVIGATING THE CHALLENGES

a. Dealing with societal pressures: Acknowledge and navigate societal pressures that may perpetuate the notion that being in a relationship is the ultimate source of happiness. Challenge these beliefs and stay true to your path and values.

b. Managing loneliness: Understand that feelings of loneliness can arise in any season of life, including singleness. Explore ways to build a supportive network, engage in meaningful connections, and practice self-soothing techniques to manage loneliness effectively.

CULTIVATING GROWTH AND TRANSFORMATION

a. Self-discovery and personal growth: View singleness as an opportunity for self-discovery and personal growth. Explore your passions, interests, and values, and invest in activities that allow you to develop new skills, broaden your perspective, and deepen your understanding of yourself.

b. Embracing transformative experiences: Embrace the transformative experiences that come with the single season. These may include facing and overcoming challenges, learning from past relationships, and embracing the opportunity for personal reinvention and renewal.

BUILDING A MEANINGFUL LIFE

a. Setting and pursuing goals: Set meaningful goals that align with your passions, values, and aspirations. Use this season to focus on personal and professional development, and create a life that brings you fulfilment and a sense of purpose.

b. Cultivating meaningful connections: Foster deep and meaningful connections with friends, family, and like-minded individuals. Surround yourself with a supportive network that encourages personal growth, shares common interests, and celebrates your journey in singleness.

EMBRACING GRATITUDE AND MINDFULNESS

a. Practicing gratitude: Cultivate a sense of gratitude for the experiences, opportunities, and lessons that come with singleness. Focus on the present moment and appreciate the abundance and beauty in your life.

b. Embracing mindfulness: Practice mindfulness to stay grounded and fully experience the joys and challenges of your journey. Be present, engage in self-reflection, and appreciate the growth and transformation that occur along the way.

Embracing the journey of thriving in singleness involves recognizing the joys, navigating the challenges, and cultivating personal growth and transformation. By celebrating the freedoms and joys of singleness, navigating societal pressures, and embracing the opportunities for self-discovery and personal development, individuals can create a meaningful and fulfilling life. Embrace the transformative experiences, cultivate gratitude and mindfulness, and build meaningful connections to fully embrace and appreciate the journey of thriving in singleness. Remember that this journey is unique and ongoing, offering endless possibilities for growth, self-fulfilment, and the creation of a life that reflects your truest self.

PART NINE

FINDING JOY AND CONTENTMENT IN THE PRESENT MOMENT

"This is the day that the Lord has made; let us rejoice and be glad in it." - Psalm 118:24

In a fast-paced and often demanding world, finding joy and contentment in the present moment has become a precious pursuit. The ancient wisdom of Psalm 118:24 reminds us of the profound truth that each day is a gift from the divine. It calls us to rejoice and be glad in the present moment, recognizing its inherent beauty and significance. By embracing a mindful and grateful approach to life, we can cultivate a deep sense of joy and contentment that transcends circumstances and allows us to fully experience the richness of each passing moment.

EMBRACING MINDFULNESS

a. Awakening to the present moment: Mindfulness involves intentionally bringing our attention to the present moment, free from judgment or attachment to the past or future. By practicing mindfulness, we open ourselves up to the fullness of life unfolding before us.

b. Cultivating awareness: Developing a heightened awareness of our thoughts, emotions, and sensations enables us to fully engage with the present moment. It allows us to savour the simple pleasures, appreciate the beauty around us, and find joy in the seemingly ordinary aspects of life.

GRATITUDE AS A GATEWAY TO JOY

a. Shifting perspective: Gratitude is a powerful mindset that can shift our focus from what is lacking to what is abundant in our lives. By consciously recognizing and appreciating the blessings, big and small, we invite joy and contentment to permeate our existence.

b. Cultivating a gratitude practice: Engaging in regular gratitude practices, such as keeping a gratitude journal or expressing appreciation to others, enhances our ability to find joy in the present moment. It trains our minds to seek out the positive and fosters a deeper sense of contentment.

LETTING GO OF ATTACHMENTS

a. Embracing impermanence: Recognizing the impermanent nature of all things frees us from the grip of attachments and expectations. When we let go of the need for things to be a certain way, we open ourselves up to the beauty and possibilities that exist in the present moment.

b. Embracing the beauty of simplicity: Simplifying our lives and letting go of excess can create space for joy and contentment to flourish. By focusing on what truly matters and releasing the unnecessary, we discover the freedom and serenity that come with living in the present.

FINDING MEANING AND PURPOSE

a. Engaging in meaningful activities: Pursuing activities aligned with our values and passions brings a profound sense of fulfilment. By engaging in activities that resonate with our souls, we infuse each moment with purpose and meaning, igniting a deep sense of joy.

b. Cultivating connections: Nurturing meaningful connections with others fosters a sense of belonging and enriches our experience of the present moment. Investing time and energy in building and nurturing relationships allows us to share and celebrate life's joys together.

In a world often consumed by busyness and future-oriented thinking, finding joy and contentment in the present moment is a transformative practice. By embracing mindfulness, cultivating gratitude, letting go of attachments, and finding meaning and purpose, we can discover a profound sense of joy and contentment that resides within us. As we reflect on the wisdom of Psalm 118:24, let us strive to rejoice and be glad in each day, recognizing the beauty, blessings, and opportunities that the present moment holds. In doing so, we unlock the true essence of living fully and experiencing joy in all its splendour.

MINDFUL EATING

Savouring the Present Moment through Nourishment

In our fast-paced and hectic lives, we often rush through meals without fully savouring the experience. However, mindful eating allows us to cultivate a deep sense of joy and contentment by embracing the present moment and nourishing our bodies and souls. By applying the principles of mindfulness to our eating habits, we can rekindle our connection with food, enhance our appreciation for nourishment, and find profound joy and contentment in the act of eating.

ENGAGING THE SENSES

a. Heightening awareness: Mindful eating involves engaging all our senses—sight, smell, touch, taste, and even sound. By tuning into these sensory experiences, we can fully immerse ourselves in the present moment and appreciate the flavours, textures, and aromas of our food.

b. Slowing down: Taking the time to eat slowly and deliberately allows us to savour each bite and fully experience the nourishment it provides. It helps us become attuned to our body's cues of hunger and satiety, promoting a healthier relationship with food.

CULTIVATING GRATITUDE

a. Appreciating the journey: Cultivating gratitude for the journey our food has taken from farm to table instils a sense of awe and reverence. Reflecting on the effort, resources, and natural processes involved in food production deepens our appreciation for the nourishment we receive.

b. Recognizing abundance: Embracing a mindset of abundance and gratitude for the food on our plate allows us to approach each meal with a sense of joy and contentment. Acknowledging the privilege of having access to nourishing food fosters a profound sense of gratitude.

BREAKING FREE FROM DISTRACTIONS

a. Minimizing distractions: Creating an environment free from distractions, such as electronic devices or work-related activities, enables us to focus solely on the act of eating. By giving our undivided attention to the present moment, we can fully enjoy the flavours and experience a deep sense of satisfaction.

b. Mindful meal rituals: Incorporating mindful meal rituals, such as saying grace, taking a moment of silence, or expressing gratitude, helps us transition into a state of presence and gratitude before beginning our meal.

NOURISHING BODY AND SOUL

a. Honouring nutritional needs: Mindful eating involves making conscious choices that honour our body's nutritional needs. By selecting nourishing foods and eating mindfully, we can enhance our overall well-being and find joy in taking care of ourselves.

b. Cultivating self-compassion: Mindful eating invites us to approach our food choices and eating habits with self-compassion. Letting go of judgment and embracing a gentle and non-judgmental attitude towards ourselves allows us to cultivate a deeper sense of joy and contentment.

Mindful eating offers a unique and transformative opportunity to find joy and contentment in the present moment. By engaging our senses, cultivating gratitude, breaking free from distractions, and nourishing our bodies and souls, we can transform the act of eating into a deeply satisfying and joyful experience. As we reflect on the wisdom of Psalm 118:24, let us embrace the present moment and rejoice in the nourishment it brings, both physically and spiritually. By practicing mindful eating, we can cultivate a profound connection with our food, foster a healthier relationship with nourishment, and discover the true joy and contentment that lie within each bite.

NATURE IMMERSION

Discovering Joy and Contentment through Connection with the Natural World

In the midst of busy schedules and modern distractions, finding joy and contentment in the present moment can be profoundly facilitated by immersing ourselves in the beauty and tranquillity of nature. Nature provides us with a sanctuary where we can escape the noise of daily life, reconnect with our senses, and experience a deep sense of joy and contentment. By embracing nature immersion, we can tap into the restorative power of the natural world and cultivate a profound connection with the present moment.

AWAKENING THE SENSES

a. Engaging with the environment: Nature immersion involves fully engaging our senses to experience the sights, sounds, smells, textures, and even tastes of the natural world around us. By intentionally immersing ourselves in nature, we awaken our senses and become fully present in the moment.

b. Heightening awareness: As we spend time in nature, we become attuned to the subtle changes in the environment, the delicate movements of wildlife, and the soothing sounds of rustling leaves or flowing water. This heightened awareness allows us to fully appreciate and find joy in the present moment.

CULTIVATING MINDFULNESS

a. Embracing stillness and silence: Nature

provides an opportunity to embrace stillness and silence, allowing us to quiet the mind and be fully present. By intentionally letting go of distractions and immersing ourselves in the serenity of nature, we cultivate mindfulness and experience a deep sense of peace and contentment.

b. Observing the rhythm of nature: By observing the natural cycles and patterns of the environment, such as the changing seasons or the rising and setting of the sun, we connect with the flow of life. This connection helps us synchronize with the present moment and find joy in the harmony and rhythm of nature.

FINDING BEAUTY AND AWE

a. Cultivating a sense of wonder: Nature has a way of inspiring awe and wonder, reminding us of the vastness and intricacy of the world we inhabit. By opening ourselves up to the beauty and majesty of nature, we tap into a sense of awe that fills us with joy and deepens our appreciation for the present moment.

b. Seeking simplicity and serenity: Nature has a way of simplifying our lives and inviting us to embrace its inherent serenity. By stepping away from the complexities of modern living and immersing ourselves in nature's simplicity, we find joy in the pure and unadorned experiences it offers.

CONNECTING WITH OUR TRUE NATURE

a. Nurturing our innate connection: As human beings, we have an innate connection with the natural world. By immersing ourselves in nature, we awaken and strengthen this connection, experiencing a profound sense of belonging and interconnectedness with all living things.

b. Letting go of time constraints: Nature operates on its own timeless rhythm, unaffected by the pressures of time that often consume our daily lives. By immersing ourselves in nature, we can release the grip of time, finding freedom and contentment in the eternal present moment.

Nature immersion offers a transformative path to finding joy and contentment in the present moment. By awakening our senses, cultivating mindfulness, embracing the beauty and awe of the natural world, and connecting with our true nature, we can experience a profound sense of joy, peace, and belonging. As we venture into the great outdoors, let us heed the wisdom of Psalm 118:24

and rejoice in the day that the Lord has made, finding solace, inspiration, and deep contentment in the beauty and harmony of the natural world.

CREATIVE EXPRESSION
Unleashing Joy and Contentment through Artistic Exploration

Creative expression provides a gateway to finding joy and contentment in the present moment. Through various forms of art, we tap into our inner selves, express our unique perspectives, and experience a profound sense of fulfilment. Engaging in creative endeavours allows us to immerse ourselves in the present, explore our passions, and discover the transformative power of self-expression. By embracing artistic exploration, we can unleash our creativity, find joy in the process, and cultivate deep contentment in the present moment.

CONNECTING WITH INNER SELF

a. Tapping into intuition: Engaging in creative expression invites us to listen to our intuition, allowing ideas and inspiration to flow freely. By tuning in to our inner selves, we connect with our authentic voice and find joy in the process of self-discovery and self-expression.

b. Embracing vulnerability: Creative expression often requires vulnerability as we share our unique perspectives and emotions through art. By embracing vulnerability, we open ourselves up to deeper connections with ourselves and others, fostering a sense of joy and contentment.

IMMERSION IN THE CREATIVE PROCESS

a. Engaging in flow: The creative process can lead us to a state of flow—a state of complete absorption and focus. When we lose ourselves in the process of creation, time seems to disappear, and we experience a profound sense of joy and contentment.

b. Embracing imperfection: The act of creation allows us to let go of perfectionism and embrace imperfections. By accepting and celebrating the unique qualities of our artistic expression, we find joy in the freedom of self-expression.

CULTIVATING MINDFULNESS

a. Presence in the process: Engaging in creative activities invites us to be fully present in the moment. As we immerse ourselves in the act of creation, we become attuned to the details, textures, colours, and sensations, enhancing our mindfulness and deepening our joy and contentment.

b. Art as meditation: Engaging in artistic pursuits can serve as a form of meditation, offering a respite from the busyness of life. By focusing our attention on the creative process, we quiet the mind, cultivate inner stillness, and find joy in the peacefulness of the present moment.

SHARING AND CONNECTING

a. Celebrating self-expression: Sharing our artistic creations with others allows us to celebrate our unique voices and perspectives. By connecting with others through our art, we foster a sense of joy, fulfilment, and a deepened sense of community.

b. Inspiring and being inspired: Engaging in creative expression not only brings us joy but also has the potential to inspire and uplift others. By sharing our art and appreciating the creations of others, we engage in a collective celebration of creativity, fostering a sense of interconnectedness and contentment.

Conclusion

Creative expression holds the power to unleash joy and contentment in the present moment. By connecting with our inner selves, immersing ourselves in the creative process, cultivating mindfulness, and sharing our artistic expressions, we embark on a transformative journey of self-discovery and self-expression. As we engage in artistic exploration, let us heed the call of Psalm 118:24 and rejoice in the day that the Lord has made, finding joy and contentment through the boundless possibilities of creative expression.

Cultivating Mindfulness:

Discovering Joy and Contentment in the Present Moment

Cultivating mindfulness is a powerful practice that allows us to fully engage with the present moment, leading to a deep sense of joy and contentment. By developing a heightened awareness of our thoughts, emotions, and surroundings, we can free ourselves from the distractions of the past and the worries of the future. Embracing mindfulness enables us to savour the richness of each moment and find profound joy and contentment in the present.

BEING FULLY PRESENT

a. Letting go of the past: Dwelling on past regrets or grievances can rob us of the joy and contentment available in the present moment. By practicing mindfulness, we learn to let go of past experiences, forgiving ourselves and others, and embracing the present with a fresh perspective.

b. Quieting the future worries: Constantly worrying about the future can overshadow our ability to find joy and contentment in the present. Mindfulness helps us cultivate a sense of trust and acceptance, allowing us to release anxiety and embrace the uncertainty of the future with calmness and equanimity.

CULTIVATING GRATITUDE

a. Noticing the blessings: Mindfulness heightens our awareness of the blessings and simple joys that surround us daily. By intentionally shifting our focus to gratitude, we recognize and appreciate the abundance and beauty present in our lives, fostering a sense of joy and contentment.

b. Gratitude practice: Engaging in regular gratitude practices, such as journaling, expressing appreciation to others, or reflecting on moments of gratitude, strengthens our ability to find joy and contentment in the present. It shifts our attention to the positive aspects of our lives, fostering a more optimistic and joyful outlook.

EMBRACING ACCEPTANCE

a. Accepting the present moment: Mindfulness invites us to accept the present moment as it is, without judgment or resistance. By letting go of the desire for things to be different, we cultivate contentment and find joy in embracing the beauty of the present reality.

b. Accepting ourselves: Self-acceptance is a key component of finding joy and contentment in the present moment. By practicing self-compassion and embracing our strengths and imperfections, we cultivate a deep sense of love and contentment within ourselves.

ENGAGING THE SENSES

a. Heightening sensory experiences:

Mindfulness involves fully engaging our senses in the present moment. By consciously savouring the sights, sounds, tastes, smells, and textures of our surroundings, we awaken to the richness and beauty of each experience, finding joy and contentment in the present.

b. Mindful activities: Engaging in activities such as mindful walking, mindful eating, or engaging in creative pursuits allows us to fully immerse ourselves in the present moment. These activities bring a heightened sense of awareness and enjoyment, leading to a profound sense of joy and contentment.

Cultivating mindfulness offers a profound pathway to finding joy and contentment in the present moment. By embracing the practice of being fully present, cultivating gratitude, embracing acceptance, and engaging our senses, we unlock the potential for profound joy and contentment in every aspect of our lives. As we reflect on the wisdom of Psalm 118:24, let us embrace mindfulness as a tool for rejoicing and finding gladness in the day that the Lord has made. Through mindfulness, we can discover the true richness and beauty of each moment, allowing joy and contentment to blossom in our lives.

CULTIVATING MINDFUL RELATIONSHIPS

Nurturing Joy and Contentment in Connection

Finding joy and contentment in the present moment extends beyond individual practices. It also involves cultivating mindful relationships and nurturing connections with others. By fostering genuine connections and deepening our presence in relationships, we can experience profound joy, fulfilment, and contentment. This sub-topic explores the power of mindful relationships in bringing us into the richness of the present moment and finding lasting happiness.

DEEP LISTENING AND PRESENCE

a. Cultivating attentive listening: Mindful relationships require active listening, where we give our full attention to others without judgment or distraction. By truly hearing and understanding others, we create a space for authentic connection and discover joy in the depth of our relationships.

b. Being fully present: Mindful relationships involve being fully present in the company of others. By consciously letting go of distractions and worries, we immerse ourselves in the present moment, deepening our connections and finding contentment in the shared experience.

CULTIVATING COMPASSION AND EMPATHY

a. Cultivating empathy: Mindful relationships thrive on empathy, where we seek to understand and share in the experiences and emotions of others. By embracing empathy, we foster deeper connections and generate a sense of joy and fulfilment through supporting and caring for one another.

b. Nurturing compassion: Compassion is at the heart of mindful relationships. By nurturing a compassionate mindset, we cultivate an environment of kindness, acceptance, and understanding, creating space for joy and contentment to flourish.

AUTHENTIC COMMUNICATION

a. Speaking with intention: Mindful relationships involve conscious and intentional communication. By choosing our words carefully, expressing ourselves honestly and respectfully, we create an atmosphere of trust and mutual understanding, paving the way for deeper joy and contentment in our connections.

b. Sharing vulnerability: Authentic and mindful relationships embrace vulnerability. By sharing our true selves, including our hopes, fears, and aspirations, we create an environment where joy and contentment can arise from genuine acceptance and support.

CULTIVATING GRATITUDE IN RELATIONSHIPS

a. Appreciating others: Mindful relationships are grounded in gratitude for the presence of others in our lives. By expressing appreciation and acknowledging the positive qualities and contributions of those around us, we nurture a culture of gratitude that fosters joy and contentment in our relationships.

b. Cherishing shared experiences: Mindful relationships value and celebrate shared experiences. By being fully present and savouring the moments we spend together, we deepen our connections and cultivate a lasting sense of joy and contentment.

Cultivating mindful relationships is a powerful way to find joy and contentment in the present moment. By practicing deep listening and presence, cultivating compassion and empathy, embracing authentic communication, and nurturing gratitude in our relationships, we create spaces where joy and contentment can thrive. As we embrace the wisdom of Psalm 118:24, let us recognize the profound joy and fulfilment that can be found in nurturing mindful relationships, rejoicing in the present moment, and being glad in the company of those who enrich our lives.

CULTIVATING MINDFUL GRATITUDE
Enhancing Joy and Contentment in Daily Life

Cultivating mindful gratitude is a transformative practice that allows us to find joy and contentment in the present moment. By shifting our focus to the blessings and abundance that surround us, we open ourselves to a deeper appreciation for life's simple pleasures. This sub-topic explores the power of mindful gratitude in enhancing our overall well-being, fostering a positive mindset, and cultivating lasting joy and contentment.

THE PRACTICE OF GRATITUDE
a. **Cultivating awareness:** Mindful gratitude

begins with developing awareness of the present moment and intentionally recognizing the blessings and positive aspects of our lives. By pausing to reflect on what we are grateful for, we shift our perspective and invite joy and contentment into our daily lives.

b. Gratitude journaling: Keeping a gratitude journal is a powerful tool for cultivating mindful gratitude. By regularly writing down the things we are grateful for, we train our minds to focus on the positive, fostering a sense of joy and contentment.

FINDING BEAUTY IN THE ORDINARY

a. Mindful observation: Embracing mindful gratitude involves consciously observing and appreciating the beauty and wonder in the ordinary moments of life. By engaging our senses and being fully present, we discover joy and contentment in the simple pleasures that often go unnoticed.

b. Practicing mindfulness in daily activities: Infusing mindfulness into our daily activities, such as eating, walking, or doing chores, allows us to fully experience and savour the present moment. By cultivating awareness and gratitude during these activities, we unlock a source of profound joy and contentment.

SHIFTING PERSPECTIVES

a. Embracing abundance: Mindful gratitude helps us shift from a mindset of scarcity to a mindset of abundance. By recognizing and appreciating what we already have, rather than focusing on what is lacking, we cultivate contentment and find joy in the richness of our lives.

b. Reframing challenges: Mindful gratitude enables us to reframe challenges and setbacks as opportunities for growth and learning. By finding gratitude even in difficult situations, we cultivate resilience, optimism, and a deeper sense of joy and contentment.

EXPRESSING AND SHARING GRATITUDE

a. Cultivating kindness: Mindful gratitude extends beyond personal reflection. By actively expressing gratitude to others and engaging in acts of kindness, we foster positive connections and create a ripple effect of joy and contentment.

b. Creating gratitude rituals: Incorporating gratitude rituals into our daily lives, such as expressing gratitude before meals or bedtime, fosters a sense of ritual and reinforces the practice of mindful gratitude. These rituals serve as reminders to pause, reflect, and cultivate joy and contentment.

Cultivating mindful gratitude is a transformative practice that allows us to find joy and contentment in the present moment. By embracing the practice of gratitude, finding beauty in the ordinary, shifting our perspectives, and expressing gratitude to others, we unlock a profound source of joy and contentment in our daily lives. As we reflect on the wisdom of Psalm 118:24, let us embrace the practice of mindful gratitude and rejoice in the day that the Lord has made, finding everlasting joy and contentment in the abundance of blessings that surround us.

LETTING GO OF ATTACHMENT

Embracing Freedom and Finding Joy in the Present Moment

Finding joy and contentment in the present moment often requires us to let go of attachments and embrace the freedom that comes with it. Attachment to outcomes, possessions, or even past experiences can prevent us from fully experiencing the present and hinder our ability to find genuine happiness. This sub-topic explores the transformative power of letting go and the path it opens towards joy and contentment in the present moment.

DETACHING FROM THE PAST

a. Releasing regrets and resentments: Dwelling on past mistakes or holding onto grudges can weigh us down and prevent us from finding joy and contentment. By practicing forgiveness, letting go of regrets, and releasing resentments, we create space for healing and experiencing the present with greater clarity and peace.

b. Embracing impermanence: Recognizing the transient nature of life allows us to let go of attachments to past experiences and embrace the beauty and possibilities of the present moment. By accepting the impermanence of life, we open ourselves to new opportunities for joy and contentment.

EMBRACING NON-ATTACHMENT

a. Letting go of expectations: Attachment to

specific outcomes or expectations can create stress and disappointment. By cultivating non-attachment and embracing the flow of life, we open ourselves to the unexpected, finding joy and contentment in the present moment regardless of the outcome.

b. Relinquishing control: Trying to control every aspect of our lives can lead to frustration and anxiety. By relinquishing control and surrendering to the natural unfolding of life, we invite a sense of ease and find joy in the freedom of letting go.

CULTIVATING MINDFUL ACCEPTANCE

a. Accepting what is: Mindful acceptance involves acknowledging and embracing the present moment as it is, without resistance or judgment. By accepting the reality of our circumstances, we find peace and contentment, allowing joy to naturally arise.

b. Embracing the power of now: The present moment is where true joy and contentment reside. By focusing our attention on the here and now, we detach from worries about the future or longing for the past, enabling us to fully engage with the present and discover the profound beauty and joy it holds.

CULTIVATING CONTENTMENT

a. Finding fulfilment within: True contentment comes from within and is not dependent on external circumstances. By shifting our focus from external achievements or possessions to cultivating inner qualities such as gratitude, compassion, and self-acceptance, we find lasting joy and contentment.

b. Practicing simplicity: Simplifying our lives by letting go of excess and embracing a more minimalist approach allows us to appreciate the present moment and the simple pleasures it offers. By reducing distractions, we create space for joy and contentment to flourish.

Finding joy and contentment in the present moment requires us to let go of attachments and embrace the freedom that comes with it. By detaching from the past, embracing non-attachment, cultivating mindful acceptance, and finding fulfilment within, we unlock the transformative power of letting go. As we journey through life, let us reflect on the wisdom of finding joy and contentment in the present moment, releasing attachments, and rejoicing in the freedom that allows us to fully experience the richness of life.

CULTIVATING MINDFULNESS

Uncovering Joy and Contentment in the Present Moment

Finding joy and contentment in the present moment is intricately connected to the practice of mindfulness. Mindfulness allows us to fully engage with the present, letting go of distractions and cultivating a deep sense of awareness and appreciation. This sub-topic explores the power of mindfulness in uncovering joy and contentment, providing practical strategies to incorporate mindfulness into our daily lives.

THE ESSENCE OF MINDFULNESS

a. Cultivating awareness: Mindfulness involves intentionally bringing our attention to the present moment, observing our thoughts, feelings, and sensations without judgment. By cultivating awareness, we develop a deeper understanding of ourselves and the world around us, opening the door to joy and contentment.

b. Embracing non-judgment: Mindfulness encourages us to let go of judgment and accept the present moment as it is, without labelling it as good or bad. By embracing non-judgment, we create space for genuine joy and contentment to arise.

MINDFUL PRESENCE

a. Engaging the senses: Mindful presence is enhanced by actively engaging our senses. By fully experiencing the sights, sounds, smells, tastes, and textures of our surroundings, we anchor ourselves in the present moment and discover joy in the richness of our sensory experiences.

b. Cultivating gratitude: Mindful presence is deeply intertwined with gratitude. By intentionally noticing and appreciating the small blessings and moments of beauty in our lives, we foster a sense of joy and contentment that arises from an attitude of gratitude.

DAILY MINDFULNESS PRACTICES

a. Mindful breathing: Practicing conscious breathing is a powerful tool to anchor ourselves in the present moment. By focusing on our breath, we bring our attention away from past or future concerns, and into the here and now, finding peace and contentment in the simplicity of each breath.

b. Mindful body scan: A body scan meditation involves systematically bringing our attention to different parts of the body, cultivating awareness and relaxation. By connecting with our bodies in the present moment, we nurture a sense of grounding and contentment.

INTEGRATING MINDFULNESS INTO DAILY LIFE

a. Mindful eating: Paying attention to the sensations, flavours, and textures while eating allows us to fully savour our meals and cultivate gratitude for nourishment. By bringing mindfulness to our eating habits, we develop a deeper connection with our food and find joy and contentment in the act of nourishing our bodies.

b. Mindful activities: Engaging in daily activities with mindfulness, such as walking, cleaning, or working, invites a sense of presence and fulfilment. By bringing our full attention to each task, we cultivate a deep appreciation for the present moment and discover joy in even the simplest of activities.

Cultivating mindfulness is a transformative

practice that enables us to uncover joy and contentment in the present moment. By embracing awareness, practicing mindful presence, incorporating daily mindfulness practices, and integrating mindfulness into our daily lives, we open ourselves to the richness of each moment. As we embrace the wisdom of finding joy and contentment in the present moment, let us embark on the journey of mindfulness, allowing it to guide us towards a deeper sense of joy, contentment, and fulfilment in all aspects of our lives.

PART TEN

EMBRACING A LIFE OF PURPOSE AND IMPACT

"But you are a chosen people, a royal priesthood, a holy nation, God's special possession, that you may declare the praises of him who called you out of darkness into his wonderful light." -
1 Peter 2:9

In the pursuit of a fulfilling and meaningful life, embracing a sense of purpose and making a positive impact holds profound significance. As stated in 1 Peter 2:9, we are reminded that we are chosen, called out of darkness into a wonderful light, entrusted with a unique role in this world. This sub-topic explores the importance of embracing a life of purpose and impact, understanding our divine calling, and discovering ways to contribute to the betterment of ourselves and the world around us.

EMBRACING YOUR DIVINE IDENTITY

Recognizing Your Worth and Cultivating Self-Belief

Embracing your divine identity is a transformative process that involves recognizing your worth as a chosen person and God's special possession. By understanding your inherent value and cultivating self-belief, you can embark on a journey of purpose and make a meaningful impact in the world. This sub-topic explores the significance of embracing your divine identity, recognizing your worth, and cultivating self-belief in fulfilling your divine calling.

RECOGNIZING YOUR WORTH

a. Embracing your chosen status: Understanding that you are chosen by God brings a profound sense of worth and significance. This recognition affirms that you have been intentionally set apart for a purpose and are deeply valued by the Creator.

b. Embracing your uniqueness: Each individual is fearfully and wonderfully made, with a set of unique gifts, talents, and abilities. Recognizing and embracing your uniqueness allows you to appreciate your worth and understand the distinctive contributions you can make in the world.

CULTIVATING SELF-BELIEF

a. Acknowledging your gifts and talents: Cultivating self-belief involves acknowledging and embracing the gifts and talents that have been bestowed upon you. Recognizing your God-given abilities allows you to have confidence in your potential to make a difference.

b. Developing a positive mindset: Cultivating self-belief requires nurturing a positive mindset. By focusing on your strengths, celebrating your achievements, and reframing negative self-talk, you can build a strong foundation of self-belief and overcome self-doubt.

EMBRACING YOUR DIVINE CALLING

a. Understanding your purpose: Embracing your divine identity involves understanding your purpose. By seeking spiritual guidance, spending time in prayer and reflection, and listening to the whispers of your heart, you can gain clarity on the unique mission and impact you are called to make.

b. Stepping into your purpose: With self-belief and an understanding of your worth, you can confidently step into your divine calling. Embrace the opportunities and challenges that come your way, knowing that you have been uniquely equipped to fulfil your purpose.

MAKING A MEANINGFUL IMPACT

a. Serving others with humility: Embracing your divine identity involves recognizing that your purpose is not self-serving but rather focused on serving others. By approaching service with humility and a genuine desire to make a positive impact, you contribute to the betterment of individuals and communities.

b. Inspiring and empowering others: As you

embrace your divine identity and fulfil your purpose, you have the power to inspire and empower others. By sharing your journey, offering encouragement, and supporting others in their paths, you create a ripple effect of positive change.

Embracing your divine identity is a transformative journey that begins with recognizing your worth and cultivating self-belief. By understanding that you are chosen and embracing your uniqueness, you can step into your divine calling with confidence and make a meaningful impact in the world. As you serve others with humility and inspire those around you, you reflect the love and light of your Creator. Embracing your divine identity allows you to fulfil your purpose and live a life of significance, contributing to a world filled with purpose and love.

DISCOVERING PERSONAL PURPOSE

Self-Reflection and Living in Alignment with Core Values

Discovering personal purpose is a transformative journey that begins with self-reflection and understanding our core values. By delving into our inner selves and aligning our actions with what truly matters to us, we can uncover our unique purpose and live a life of fulfilment and meaning. This sub-topic explores the importance of self-reflection and identifying personal values in discovering and living in alignment with our purpose.

SELF-REFLECTION FOR PURPOSE

a. Creating space for introspection: Embracing a life of purpose starts with creating time and space for introspection. This can involve practices such as journaling, meditation, or quiet contemplation, allowing us to delve into our thoughts, feelings, and aspirations.

b. Exploring passions and strengths: Self-reflection entails exploring our passions and strengths. By identifying the activities and topics that energize and bring us joy, as well as recognizing our unique talents and skills, we gain insights into the areas where our purpose may lie.

UNCOVERING CORE VALUES

a. Understanding the importance of values: Core values represent what is most important and meaningful to us. They serve as guiding principles that shape our decisions and actions. By recognizing the significance of values, we can align our lives with what truly matters.

b. Reflecting on personal values: Taking time to reflect on our personal values helps us understand what resonates with our authentic selves. This can involve asking ourselves questions such as "What do I prioritize in my life?" or "What principles do I hold dear?"

LIVING IN ALIGNMENT WITH PURPOSE

a. Aligning actions with values: Once we have identified our core values, it is essential to align our actions with them. By making conscious choices that reflect our values, we create a life that is in harmony with what is most important to us.

b. Seeking opportunities that align with purpose: Living in alignment with purpose involves seeking out opportunities and experiences that resonate with our values and passions. By actively pursuing endeavours that reflect our authentic selves, we contribute to a sense of fulfilment and meaning.

EMBRACING GROWTH AND ADAPTATION

a. Embracing personal growth: The journey of discovering personal purpose is not static but rather an ongoing process of growth and self-development. By embracing opportunities for learning, expanding our skills, and challenging ourselves, we evolve along our purposeful path.

b. Allowing flexibility and adaptation: As we navigate the discovery of our purpose, it is important to remain open to change and adaptation. Our understanding of purpose may evolve over time, and being flexible allows us to align with new insights and experiences.

Discovering personal purpose is a transformative endeavour that starts with self-reflection and living in alignment with our core values. By creating space for introspection, exploring our passions and strengths, and identifying our values, we gain valuable insights into our unique purpose. As we align our actions with our values and embrace personal growth, we embark on a journey of fulfilment, meaning, and impact. By delving into self-reflection and embracing our core values, we uncover the path that leads us to a purposeful and meaningful life.

LIVING WITH INTENTION

Setting Meaningful Goals and Making Purpose-Aligned Choices

Living with intention is a transformative way of approaching life, cantered around setting meaningful goals and making choices that align with your divine calling. By establishing clear objectives and consciously aligning your actions with your purpose, you create a sense of direction, fulfilment, and impact in your daily life. This sub-topic explores the significance of living with intention, setting meaningful goals, and making purpose-aligned choices to fulfil your divine calling.

SETTING MEANINGFUL GOALS

a. Identifying your values and priorities: Setting meaningful goals begins with understanding your core values and priorities. By aligning your goals with what matters most to you, you create a sense of purpose and fulfilment.

b. SMART goal-setting: Utilizing the SMART (Specific, Measurable, Achievable, Relevant, Time-bound) framework helps in setting clear and actionable goals. This approach ensures that your goals are specific, measurable, attainable, relevant to your purpose, and bound by a specific timeframe.

MAKING PURPOSE-ALIGNED CHOICES

a. Reflecting on the impact of choices: Recognizing that every choice has the potential to either support or divert you from your purpose is crucial. By considering the potential consequences and aligning choices with your divine calling, you ensure that your actions contribute to your desired impact.

b. Practicing discernment and alignment: Making purpose-aligned choices requires discernment and a deep understanding of your values and purpose. Regular self-reflection, prayer, and seeking guidance can help you make choices that align with your divine calling.

EMBRACING MINDFUL DECISION-MAKING

a. Cultivating self-awareness: Mindful decision-making involves cultivating self-awareness. By being attuned to your thoughts, emotions, and motivations, you can make choices that are in alignment with your purpose and values.

b. Considering long-term consequences: Mindful decision-making involves considering the long-term consequences of your choices. By evaluating how your decisions may impact your personal growth, relationships, and overall sense of fulfilment, you can make choices that align with your greater purpose.

MAINTAINING FOCUS AND ACCOUNTABILITY

a. Regular review and reflection: Living with intention requires regular review and reflection on your goals and choices. By assessing your progress, adjusting course when needed, and celebrating milestones, you maintain focus and stay accountable to your purpose.

b. Surrounding yourself with support: Building a support system of like-minded individuals who understand and support your purpose is essential. Seek out mentors, join communities, or engage in accountability partnerships to stay motivated and encouraged on your intentional living journey.

Living with intention is a powerful approach to life, guiding you to set meaningful goals and make purpose-aligned choices. By understanding your values, setting clear objectives, and consciously aligning your actions with your divine calling, you create a life filled with direction, fulfilment, and impact. Through mindful decision-making, self-awareness, and maintaining focus, you navigate your path with purpose and align your choices with your desired impact. As you live with intention, you embrace the transformative power of purpose and contribute to a world that reflects your divine calling.

MAKING AN IMPACT

Serving Others and Inspiring Empowerment

Making an impact is a fundamental aspect of living a purposeful life. It involves selflessly serving others and inspiring and empowering them to discover their purpose. By extending kindness, compassion, and support, you can make a positive difference in the lives of others and reflect the love and light of God. This sub-topic explores the significance of serving others and inspiring empowerment as ways to make a lasting impact.

SERVING OTHERS

a. Selfless acts of kindness: Making an impact

starts with selfless acts of kindness. By extending a helping hand, volunteering, or engaging in acts of service, you demonstrate love and compassion towards those in need.

b. Meeting tangible and emotional needs: Serving others involves addressing both tangible and emotional needs. It may include providing material resources, offering a listening ear, or offering comfort and support during challenging times.

INSPIRING EMPOWERMENT

a. Sharing your story: Your personal journey and experiences have the power to inspire and uplift others. By sharing your story authentically, you can encourage individuals to pursue their dreams, overcome obstacles, and find their purpose.

b. Offering guidance and support: Empowering others means offering guidance and support along their journey. By providing mentorship, sharing insights, and offering encouragement, you can help individuals realize their potential and navigate their paths of purpose.

CULTIVATING CONNECTION AND COMMUNITY

a. Creating meaningful connections: Making an impact involves fostering genuine connections with others. By cultivating relationships built on trust, empathy, and mutual support, you create a sense of belonging and foster a supportive community.

b. Collaborating for a greater impact: Collaborating with like-minded individuals or organizations amplifies the impact you can make. By joining forces and combining resources and talents, you can tackle larger-scale challenges and create positive change together.

LEADING BY EXAMPLE

a. Living a purpose-driven life: Making an impact begins with living a purpose-driven life yourself. By embodying your values, pursuing your passions, and embracing your divine calling, you inspire others to do the same.

b. Modelling kindness and compassion: Leading by example involves modelling kindness, compassion, and empathy in your interactions with others. By demonstrating these qualities, you create a ripple effect of positivity and inspire others to follow suit.

Making an impact is a transformative way of living

that involves serving others selflessly and inspiring empowerment. By extending kindness and compassion, and by sharing your story and offering support, you make a positive difference in the lives of others. Cultivating connection and community, and leading by example, create an environment where individuals are encouraged to pursue their purpose and contribute to a greater good. Through your actions and intentions, you reflect the love and light of God, making the world a better place one act of service and inspiration at a time.

THE SALVATION MESSAGE

4 STEPS TO SALVATION.

Dear Friend,

I am so grateful to God for the opportunity He has granted us to meet through this book. I understand how difficult it may be for you to give your life to God.

Everyone knows their weak point. In the closet try and identify your weaknesses and work on them immediately. Don't wait for tomorrow because it may be too late. Face that problem now and claim your miracles. Funny enough our sin is usually what makes us to come short of the glory of God.

I am using myself as an example because today I have endless testimonies.

Salvation is the only way to enjoy the work of the almighty in totality. If you give your life to Jesus Christ and accept Him as your lord and personal saviour, it is the fastest and surest key to stepping into that "wonderful Destiny" He has in store for you. Are you tired of the things not working out for you? Are you tired of always having your own way? Why not surrender to Jesus today as you take these steps of faith...

STEP 1   CONFESS YOUR SINS

'He that covereth his sins shall not prosper: but whoso confesseth and forsaketh them shall have mercy.' (Proverbs 28:13).

STEP 2 : ASK GOD TO FORGIVE YOU

'If we confess our sins, he is faithful and just to forgive us our sins, and to cleanse us from all unrighteousness.' (1 John 1:9).

STEP 3: INVITE HIM INTO YOUR LIFE

'Behold, I stand at the door, and knock: if any man hear my voice, and open the door, I will come to him, and will sup with him, and he with me.' (Rev. 3:20).

STEP 4 : RECEIVE HIM BY FAITH

'But as many as received him, to them gave HE power to become the sons of God, even to them that believe on his name.' (John 1:12).

Please pray with me....

Dear Lord JESUS, today I come to you as a sinner, I confess my sins, forgive me and cleanse me.

Wash me with your precious blood. I invite you into my life today, even as I make you my personal Lord and SAVIOUR. I receive the gift of eternal life. I am BORN AGAIN. Thank you JESUS for accepting me and saving me now. Amen.

WELCOME TO GOD'S FAMILY.

As you are aware, every plant needs water for growth and vitality, without which it would die. As a fresh Christian, you need spiritual nutrients to keep you alive, full of vitality and victory. You need to be where like-minded people are.

You may say 'I don't want to go to Church because I don't want to be known as such a church person' but do you know that a student is not identified as such unless he is part of a class? A child cannot claim to be a member of a family if he is not part of it. So also, you need to be around Christians if you say you are one, and the best place to find them is in Church.

As LONG as the branch stays connected to the tree, it will stay alive. As long as the baby stays close to the mother, he will have what to eat. As long as you stay connected to other believers, you will not be tempted to fall back into sin, deprivation and discouragement.

Join a Bible-believing church where you can grow in the word of God as you listen to quality teachings; learn how to pray; and get to meet with other Christians who can encourage you.

BACK TO THE BEGINNING

You are now born again. What does this mean? How will it change your life?

What does it mean to receive JESUS?

You have made peace with GOD. You have a new relationship with GOD, your father, reconciled by the blood of JESUS. (John 10:10).

Like the prodigal son, you have finally come home (Luke

15:24).

You have been saved from sin, addiction, fear, guilt and shame. On the cross, JESUS paid it all for you (Romans 8:1). You are now a member of the largest gathering on earth-the people of GOD
(1 Peter 2:10).

DO YOU KNOW THAT...

When you became a Christian the ownership of your life changes hands? In the past, you were the boss doing things the way you felt like...

In the past, the devil could toss you around, bending your life out of shape whenever he felt like, hindering your blessings whenever it pleased him...

Now, you have a new boss. You have received JESUS, and HE is now in charge. HE is the sole determiner of your destiny. HE is your Guide, your fortress, your shield, your help, your Deliverer. HE is your Christ. (Romans 10:9).

FREQUENTLY ASKED QUESTIONS

How can I know that GOD has forgiven me?   (1 John 1: 8-9)

How can I know that I have eternal life?   (John 5:24)

How can I know that GOD is with me?   (John 6:37, Hebrews 13:5)

How can I know that GOD hears me?   (Jeremiah 29: 12-13)

DO YOU KNOW THAT...

You have access to divine power designed to bring victory, deliverance and prosperity into your life. You no longer need to be burdened by sin, sorrow and Satan.

You can be set free from curses, evil covenants, satanic embargoes, limitations and so on. All you need to do is move on the next stage, which is to submit yourself for proper deliverance in a Bible-believing church so that the shackles of Satan can be shattered forever out of your life, marriage, finances, career, health, academics and so on.

I want to hear from you, write me on abayendi@gmail.com

The author:

PROPHET ABRAHAM DOLLAR AYENDI

An Apostolic Prophet, founder and general overseer of Zion Embassy (Christ church), a fast growing church Network with ministry branches in Ireland, South Africa, United Kingdom, Nigeria, Canada and Singapore. He is the C.E.O of Zion publishing house.

He is a dedicated Social Worker by training and a Community champion. Prophet Abraham as he is fondly called is also the founding president of www.yourfamilyfm.com, Family Fm (your Family community radio station 94.3) and the Principal of www.globalfamilyhealthcare.com headquartered in

Dublin, Republic of Ireland.

An ardent Scholar, he holds a Post Graduate Diploma and a Masters degree in Social Care and Social Justice from Atlantic Technological University, Sligo, Republic of I r e l a n d .

A revivalist and international conference speaker with divers signs and wonders following his ministrations.

A prolific writer and author of several books including:

- NEVER GIVE UP
- DON'T SETTLE FOR LESS
- YOU CAN SUCCEED
- THE POWER OF PRAYER
- QUIET TIME
- WATCHMAN
- NEW LIFE
- HOW TO LOVE YOURSELF
- IN LOVE WITH GOD
- SINGLES MINGLES
- I WANT TO GET MARRIED
- HAPPILY MARRIED AFTER
- HOW TO KNOW HE LOVES YOU
- HOW DO I KNOW SHE LOVES ME
- TRUE LOVE
- PASTOR: YOU CAN SUCCEED.

- LETS TALK ABOUT SEX
- BEFORE I SAY I DO
- SINGLE AGAIN
- DEALING WITH DIVORCE
- CHILDREN IN DIVORCE
- OVERCOMING ANXIETY
- DEALING WITH DEPRESSION
- MAKING MONEY ONLINE
- HOW TO MAKE GOOD MONEY
- STARTING A BUSINESS
- DISCIPLINE
- MIRACLES NOW
- NO MORE INSTABILITY
- OVERCOMING GRIEF
- NEW DAD
- NEW MUM
- RAISING TEANAGE GIRLS
- RAISING TEANAGE BOYS
- RAISING GODLY CHILDREN
- FULFILLING YOUR CALLING
- HOW TO KNOW HE IS CHEATING
- HOW TO KNOW SHE IS CHEATING
- HOW TO BUILD MARRIAGE THAT WILL LAST FORVER
- HOW TO LOVE YOUR WIFE

- SUBMISSION IN MARRIAGE
- HOW TO LOVE YOUR HUSBAND
- INVESTMENT BIBLE
- UNDERSTANDING WISDOM
- RADICAL FAITH
- MENTAL HEALTH

ABOUT THE AUTHOR

Abraham Dollar is a dedicated Social Worker by training and a Community champion. Prophet Abraham as he is fondly called is also the founding president of www.yourfamilyfm.com, Family Fm (your Family community radio station 94.3) and the Principal of www.globalfamilyhealthcare.com headquartered in Dublin, Republic of Ireland. A revivalist and international conference speaker with divers signs and wonders following his ministrations.

ABOUT THE AUTHOR

Abraham Dollar is a transformative preacher of the gospel, as well as the CEO of Zion Publishing House. With a background in social care work, he is a dedicated professional and a true community champion. Not only is he the founding president of Your Family FM (www.yourfamilyfm.com), a community radio station broadcasting on 94.3 FM, but he is also the principal of Global Family Healthcare (www.globalfamilyhealthcare.com), which is headquartered in Dublin, Republic of Ireland.

Abraham Dollar is an ardent scholar, having completed a Post Graduate Diploma and a Masters degree in Social Care and Social Justice from Atlantic Technological University in Sligo, Republic of Ireland. His commitment to academic excellence and his passion for addressing social issues shine through in his work.

As a revivalist and international conference speaker, Abraham Dollar's powerful ministry is accompanied by diverse signs and wonders. His profound ability to inspire and bring about positive change has captivated audiences around the world.

Abraham Dollar truly embodies the essence of a dedicated preacher, a social care professional, and a community leader. Through his various roles and accomplishments, he continues to make a significant impact on society and uplift those around him.

ABOUT THE BOOK

"Single and Satisfied: Embracing the Power of Being Single" redefines singleness as a state of independence, freedom, and self-discovery. It embraces the idea that being single is not a mere absence of a romantic partner but rather an opportunity for personal growth, self-love, and the pursuit of one's passions. This book recognizes the inherent strength and value of being single and aims to shift the narrative to one of empowerment and fulfillment.

You are invited to embark on this transformative journey of self-discovery, personal growth, and spiritual empowerment through biblical wisdom and inspirational guidance.

Printed in Great Britain
by Amazon

25603927R00202